Artful Machine Embroidery

*A Visual Guide to Creating Clothing
You'll Love to Wear*

Bobbi Bullard

Text and Photography copyright © 2012 by Bobbi Bullard

Photography and Artwork copyright © 2012 by C&T Publishing, Inc.

Publisher: Amy Marson

Creative Director: Gailen Runge

Art Director: Kristy Zacharias

Editor: Lynn Koolish

Technical Editors: Sandy Peterson and Alison Schmidt

Cover/Book Designer: April Mostek

Production Coordinator: Zinnia Heinzmann

Production Editor: Alice Mace Nakanishi

Illustrator: Aliza Shalit

Photo Assistant: Cara Pardo

Garment Photography by Christina Carty-Francis and Diane Pedersen of C&T Publishing, Inc., unless otherwise noted; How-To Photography by Randy Bullard unless otherwise noted

Published by C&T Publishing, Inc., P.O. Box 1456, Lafayette, CA 94549

Library of Congress Cataloging-in-Publication Data

Bullard, Bobbi, 1951-

Artful machine embroidery : a visual guide to creating clothing you'll love to wear / Bobbi Bullard.

pages cm

ISBN 978-1-60705-582-2 (soft cover)

1. Embroidery, Machine--Patterns. I. Title.

TT772.B85 2012

746.44028--dc23

2012013360

Printed in China

10 9 8 7 6 5 4 3 2 1

Contents

CD Contents

For bonus machine embroidery design files
for *Artful Machine Embroidery*, see the CD.

Summary of CD files:
"Read Me" instructions
Appliqué designs (2)
Border designs (6, including a variety of lengths)
Lace designs (3)
Motif designs (6)
Reverse appliqué designs (1)
Richelieu designs (2)

Acknowledgments

Just as it takes a village to raise a child, it took a community to help me write this book. Luckily, I have such a community around me. I owe so many wonderful, giving people so much.

First, a thank-you to the bevy of women who have helped me sew the samples in this book—Jeannie McKinney, Marcia Russell, Tamara Savoca, Tecla Shaffer, Cindy Shamrock, Karen Starkel, and Doris Woods—and who have all spent many, many days sewing for me, putting their own lives on hold to do this work.

And a thank-you to Roseanne Lauters, who shared the wonderful workroom in her store to host sew-ins.

Thank you to the attendees of the sew-ins at Roseanne's store. In the spirit of quilting circles of old, they assembled to help me out. I'm sure I can't name them all, but here's a try: Adrienne Anderson, Twyla Gossack, Linda Hansen, Jan Hopkins, Betsy Kerr, Arlette Peterson, Deb Prophet-Abney, Margit Reichner, Karen Rinneli, and Pat Skaggs joined these sessions.

Anita Marshall is my personal fitting guru and has ensured that all my clothing looks as beautiful on as it does on the hanger.

The color wheel shown in this book was designed by Tecla Shaffer and constructed by Karen Starkel. Thank you for letting me use your beautiful piece.

I have a large number of personal cheerleaders whose support has kept me going, including (but not limited to) Jen Dulyanai, Suzanne Egger, Roberta Kitowski, C. Jaye Kline, Jenny Lyon, and Tecla Shaffer.

Thank you to the stalwart group who gave unselfishly of their time to read and reread the text for this book. They read, they questioned, they corrected, and most important of all, they supported me. Thank you to my dear friends Jacki McNeil and Cindy Shamrock; my sister, Carol; and her daughter, Sara (the best niece in the world). To all these people I give my heartfelt thanks.

Last but not least, a thank-you to my husband, Randy, who put up with weeks of my nonpresence when I locked myself behind closed doors and pounded away on a keyboard.

Getting It Right

I admit it: One of my highest priorities when sewing is to create something beautiful. When creating clothing, I have a secondary goal: to create something that makes me look more beautiful. Why waste my time producing something ordinary? That makes no sense to me.

—*Bobbi Bullard*

Using Your Designs to Make Art

Last year, after teaching my Design University class, I was approached by a lovely lady wearing a graceful jacket covered with stamped motifs, embroidered designs, and a sprinkling of beading. She spoke quietly but with conviction.

"I took your class last year, this class, and I want you to know that it changed my life."

Changed her life? That's quite a statement. I expect that my students will leave my class knowing a little more than when they came in, understanding what makes good design, feeling comfortable with the concepts presented, and having enough knowledge and confidence to start applying those concepts to their own work. But changing their lives? I wasn't expecting that.

"Yes," she said. "Before your class, I was convinced that I didn't have a creative bone in my body. I always started with kits or copied others' work. After taking your class, I realized that I don't have to get it right the first time, that I can play around until I like something. Now I'm comfortable trying new things. My work has improved about 1,000 percent. I wanted to thank you."

Design, good or otherwise, consists of two parts: the elements you use and the way you use them. In the next two chapters, we'll examine both the elements of design and the way you organize them to produce a beautiful finished piece.

Credits for the embroidery designs are included with their photos, and most are found on my website: www.bullarddesigns.com.

The Elements of Design

When creating a piece of fiber art, it helps to know and understand the design elements available to you—the building blocks of design. Just as an architect has to know the best materials to construct a structure, you should know the materials available for your creation. You have been using these elements all along, but identifying and classifying them will help you understand the role each plays in your overall creation.

Line

Although it seems that lines are simple, they're invaluable in design. Lines can add character, move the eye, or act as a focal point. Lines can be straight or curved, graceful or ungraceful, or even or uneven in width. Lines can converge, run parallel, or intersect. They can be playful or staid.

We don't think of lines as an important part of wearable art, yet a line can serve a variety of purposes in your garment. A line can be used as the focal point of the design; it can create movement, separate parts, or define areas of your piece.

Each line has a character of its own. Think advertising. There are companies that depend on line for identity. For example, anywhere you go in the world, regardless of language or alphabet, you'll know that a bottle is filled with Coca-Cola because of the line under the first character on the label. The words can be written in any alphabet—it doesn't matter—that graceful swoop under the first letter lets you know.

Speaking of swoops, the folks at Nike are so comfortable with a beautiful line as an identifying mark that they don't even add letters! The local alphabet doesn't matter because they don't use an alphabet at all. They rely on the line to convey the message of forward movement and excitement.

Just as these companies use lines to convey a message, we, too, use lines in our work.

Adornments—embroidery designs by author

Lines as the focal point This red jacket depends on vertical embroidery lines and Ultrasuede trim lines to send a bold message—the wearer of this garment is strong and wants you to know it.

Crystal Treasures—embroidery designs by author

Spring Delights (retired set)— embroidery designs by author

Lines to frame elements The lines in this shirt, created with decorative stitching, are a dominant part of the design, separating the flowers and allowing each one to make a statement yet be a part of the overall design.

Lines as a border These lines are made up of designs emphasizing the edges of the jacket. A line consisting of interrupted individual motifs is softer and less structured than a line of decorative stitching or bias trim.

Lines to unify This jacket is constructed from a variety of fabrics ranging from a cool, deep red to warm mango, colors that don't work well when placed next to each other. The dividing lines allow the various colors to work in harmony.

Crested Beaut—embroidery designs by author

Swirleys—embroidery designs by author

Lines that create movement How often are we told, "Wear vertical lines to draw the eye up and down"? Stripes are not the only up-and-down lines. Create the vertical lines with embellishments.

Lines that separate sections The lines in this jacket play an important role, segregating the various sections.

Deco Delights (retired set)— embroidery designs by author

Lines that create interest This wrap includes two lines. The first is a stripe of pale pink fabric. The second is a line consisting of multiple motifs. The two lines together create interest as well as serving to move the eye around the piece.

Brilliants—embroidery designs by author

Embroidered fabric with large motifs placed symmetrically
The motifs are strong by themselves but are still integrated into the total design. Using a large number of motifs limits the importance of each one.

Whimsey—embroidery designs by author

Motifs that make a statement
Larger motifs placed symmetrically down the front of a purchased shirt create a statement.

Savannah—embroidery designs by author

Motif

Also known as a *shape*, a motif not only stands on its own but is a building block for the creation of other elements. A single motif can be a focal point—a place to focus interest. Multiple motifs form patterns, textures, and lines.

One Is Not Enough

I find that the first inclination among machine embroiderers is to find a beautiful, elaborate embroidery design and center it in the middle of the chest. This is my least favorite use of machine embroidery. That single big design in the middle of my chest transforms me from human being to canvas. It invites people to come up and stare right at my chest, and it minimizes the other design elements.

One of my goals in sewing is to create items that not only look great but make me look great. To eliminate that human-turned-to-canvas effect, I almost always use multiple motifs to make my statement.

Zelda—embroidery designs by author

Motifs placed symmetrically on the jacket back
Careful placement of the motifs adds interest to this
piece. The cut of the classic jean jacket is emphasized
by replacing the back panel with embroidered fabric of
a contrasting color. Notice how the perfect symmetry of
the design panels matches the symmetry of the jacket.

Multiple motifs combined to appear as one
Here, the arrangement of motifs creates movement
and excitement. Each design is beautiful, but the
overall arrangement is important as well. If the motifs
had been more literal, for example, a realistic picture
of a flower arrangement or an animal, this design
might have strayed into the area of clothing trans-
formed into a canvas. Instead, the overall look is that
of a beautiful woman wearing a beautiful garment.

Brilliants—embroidery designs by author

Regular, irregular, and line patterns Different types of patterns create different impressions. The bottom panel has a regular pattern made up of multiple motifs. The middle panel has a random, irregular pattern. The top panel has a pattern made of regular lines. The horizontal lines in the garment serve to keep each section visually contained.

Leaf Lines—embroidery designs by author

Regular pattern
The regular pattern on this top creates a comfortable feeling. The complexity of each of the designs keeps the overall look interesting.

Botanical Jewels—embroidery designs by author

Pattern

Pattern is the most commonly forgotten design element. It is not included in most design books, yet pattern is one of the most important elements when you're considering designing your own fabric.

The definition of pattern is "a discernible, coherent system based on the intended interrelationship of component parts," which is a fancy way of saying using multiple elements to form an overall design. For our purposes, a pattern is a system of motifs arranged over a visible area.

Patterns can be regular or irregular. A regular pattern is soothing because it is predictable. It is a great way to fill in space. An irregular pattern adds excitement, movement, and interest.

Lines & Flowers—embroidery designs by author

Irregular pattern The random placement of designs creates a casual effect.

Regular pattern Each motif is a short, straight line placed in a regular pattern.

Crystal Treasures—embroidery designs by author

Crown Jewels—embroidery designs by author

Texture

Because we fiber artists work with materials that have exquisite textures of their own, we have an advantage over artists in most other media. Consider a lovely bouclé or a rich velvet, a nice crisp organza or a rigid corduroy. All we have to do to vary the texture is pull out the next piece of fabric.

Or we can use an embroidery machine to create our own texture. Multiple design motifs (either identical or not) placed close together create a textured fabric. Another way to add texture is by adding lines of stitching and creating faux chenille.

Texture adds interest and helps define the overall mood of a piece. A soft, fluffy texture such as a brushed flannel is a cozy, comfortable fiber piece. Hard edges, such as those of wool twill or organza, add formality.

Texture is such an inherent part of fiber art that we often overlook what it can add to our projects. Consciously think about using the fabric's texture as a part of your design.

Add Texture, Add Interest

One of my favorite guilty pleasures is watching home-decorator shows. Inevitably, sometime during the show, the host or hostess tosses a chenille throw across a sofa and mentions in a serious voice that he or she has saved the room by adding interest through texture.

No matter what the medium, texture is an important element, creating contrast or adding interest. In sculpture, texture is accomplished through uneven surfaces. In paintings and drawings, texture is simulated through the use of crosshatching or a large number of small dots.

To Chenille, or Not to Chenille

I love vending and teaching at sewing and quilt shows, especially when I see customers and students wearing examples of the concepts I teach or even my embroidery designs.

At one show, one of my favorite students shared her latest creation, a faux chenille jacket with added appliqué designs. Wonderful! I was in awe. First I complimented her on her fortitude. She had chenilled the fabric for a long jacket, something well beyond my attention span. Then I focused on the appliqués.

"How did you do it?" I asked her. "How did you get such a smooth appliqué over that bumpy textured surface?"

She laughed. "It was nothing," she said. "I added the appliqué before I cut through the channels and fluffed the chenille."

I loved the look so much that I created my copper-colored silk blouse (above right), adding my take on the appliqué-over-chenille technique.

Faux chenille as texture
Panels of faux chenille sport appliquéd embroidery designs. The designs were added after the lines for the faux chenille were stitched but before the channels were cut open. The small, smooth areas give the eye a place to rest, adding interest.

Brilliants—embroidery designs by author

Fabric as texture
This rich bouclé adds interest to a jacket with simple lines. The small designs give the feel of subtle jewelry.

Whimsey—embroidery designs by author

Planes

In art, planes are large open spaces, such as the sides of barns, open fields, or fences (identified as "large shapes" in some curricula). They fill a literal need—portraying a fence or field in a landscape—and fill a visual need by giving the eye a place to rest.

Quilters use planes as their most frequent building block. Planes are less popular in garments but are not unknown. There are times when negative space—which can also be considered a plane—is important.

Think about the chenille with the appliqués (page 16). Each appliqué is a small plane, a place for the eye to rest.

Block prints
In this pieced top, each pieced fabric shape is a plane. The line of embroidery spanning the separate planes brings unity to the pieces.

Flying High—embroidery designs by author

Color

Color theory is a set of principles that help you select aesthetically pleasing color combinations and set an overall tone for a piece, from exciting and vibrant to serene and earthy, or anything in between. Designers find it useful to understand the principles of color theory, the standard color vocabulary, the color wheel, and color harmony combinations. Wearable art artists use color (and all the elements of design) differently than do quiltmakers, fine artists, interior designers, and graphic artists. The successful fiber artist masters the basics while learning when to break the color theory rules for his or her own artistic effect.

The main purpose of a piece determines color choice. The graphic artist chooses bright orange and yellow for a detergent box to capture attention on a grocery store shelf; the interior designer chooses warm greens and cream for a room devoted to relaxation. Quilt artists and fine artists enjoy more latitude with color combinations—they can use any color combination in the color theory books. For wearable art, the color rules need to be tempered by the goal of wearability and the best choices to flatter the wearer.

Choosing Colors

Color theory information is readily, perhaps overly, available through books, magazine articles, websites, blogs, classes, and more. Despite that fact, almost every fiber artist has felt overwhelmed when choosing colors.

Making clothing does nothing to simplify choosing colors. In fact, it adds even more wild cards: seasonal colors, color trends, and the whims of fashion. And don't forget a key ingredient to color success—finding colors to flatter the wearer.

Color Terminology

Understanding the standard vocabulary of color makes it easier to understand the concepts of color theory.

Primary Colors

The three primary colors are *red*, *yellow*, and *blue*. In paint, the primaries are mixed together to create the other colors.

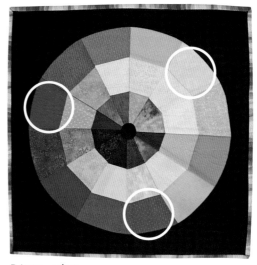

Primary colors

Secondary Colors

The three secondary colors are *orange*, *green*, and *purple*. In paint, the secondaries are created by mixing together two primary colors.

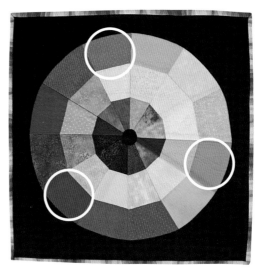

Secondary colors

Tertiary Colors

Tertiary colors are any of the six colors that, in paint, are made from mixing a primary color with a secondary color next to it on the color wheel. For example, the tertiary color *yellow-orange* is made from the primary color yellow mixed with the secondary color orange.

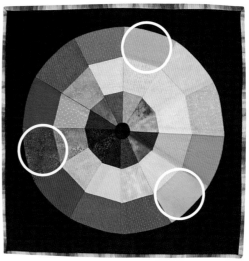

Tertiary colors

The Color Wheel

The color wheel is a common vehicle for explaining color theory and showing color relationships and combinations. It starts with the three primary colors arranged in an equilateral triangle. The secondary color made with two primary colors is placed between those two primary colors. The tertiary colors are placed between the primary and secondary colors.

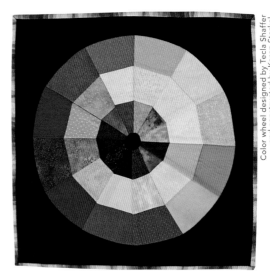

Color wheel designed by Tecla Shaffer and constructed by Karen Starkel.

The color wheel

ADDING DIMENSIONS OF COLOR

A more complex color wheel includes variations of each of the colors previously shown. Each ring of the wheel shows variants of the original color modified by adding white, black, or each color's complementary color. One ring includes colors made lighter by adding white (tints). Another ring has darkened versions of the colors (shades). Some color wheels include rings with colors that are less clear, or muddied (see Saturation, page 20).

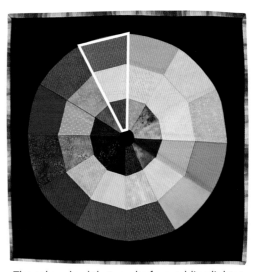

The color wheel that results from adding lighter and darker dimensions has a wedge for each color that includes its two variations. Color wheels can be as simple as the one shown or very complex.

Hue

The *hue* of a color is its most basic descriptor, such as *green*, *yellow*, or *orange*. Hue includes variations of the color as it is changed by lightening, darkening, or reducing brightness. The hue orange, for example, includes variations such as coral or umber.

Value

The *value* of a color is the degree of lightening or darkening of a hue. Pink and burgundy are the same hue—red—in different values.

Tint

In paints, *tints* are colors whose values have been lightened by adding white (when using lights or other media, different methods are used to change color values). Pastel colors are tints. Pink is a tint of the hue red.

Shade

Shades are the opposite of tints; they are colors whose values have been darkened by adding black. Burgundy is a shade of the hue red.

Saturation

Saturation is the relative brightness or dullness of a color. In the red section of the color wheel, the clear, bright red is the most saturated. A salmon pink would be the light, muddied, less saturated version. A dark, brownish burgundy is a darker version of the less saturated color.

It's All Muddy to Me

Until recently, I had undervalued the importance of saturation as a color property. In retrospect, I realize I had misunderstood the whole concept. I had been misled by definitions like "the purity of the color," "the vividness or intensity of the color," and other vague descriptions.

At the same time as I was blithely dismissing saturation, I was lecturing about the possibilities of using "muddied or toned-down colors," thinking I had defined some elusive color concept. Although I hadn't found references to muddied colors in color theory books, I explained how sage, salmon, denim blue, and other muddied, or subtle, colors make a statement in clothes. I noted that to produce a muddied color, you added some of the color's complementary color. Add a little orange to blue to create denim blue. Add red to a pale green and—*Voilà!*—sage green.

Only when I found a definition of *saturation* that I could understand did I realize that saturation explains my "muddied" colors. Suddenly, the concept of muddied colors, and their place on the color wheel, became clear. I resigned myself to the fact that I was not some great innovator in color theory.

The less saturated (or desaturated) colors create a beautiful look on this coat covered with embroidery in muted colors.

Eastern Visions—embroidery designs by author

So much of working with color theory depends on taste and mood. One designer embraces only vibrant (saturated) colors, appreciating their powerful personalities. She considers the less saturated colors dull and vague.

The next designer appreciates the subtlety of the less saturated colors, complementing their delicacy, creating tranquil effects.

In addition to using a palette of only vibrant colors or only subtle colors, you can mix the two. When combining saturated and desaturated colors, be aware that saturated colors have a much greater presence than desaturated ones. Bright red feels more important than denim blue. Using a high ratio of denim blue to red will give the two colors equal amounts of attention and create aesthetic balance.

Very Subtle

I was introduced to desaturated colors in the early 1990s, when I had my colors "done" by a color specialist who worked with a palette beyond the usual "seasons" approach to color style. First, she found color swatches that matched my hair and eye color. Then she sorted through an enormous number of swatches, pulling out colors that enhanced and flattered my eye and skin colors. She then assembled her masterpiece, colors that would highlight my attributes, an array that included coral, sage green, tans, and browns. I was crestfallen.

"All those colors are so dull," I said (insert suitably whiny voice here).

She answered, "They're not dull; they're subtle."

The moral of the story is that she was right. Those colors do look good on me. Now I seek out the dull—excuse me—subtle colors when sewing for myself. The desaturated colors have become very important to me.

Color Temperature

Another way to categorize colors is to divide them into warm and cool families.

Warm colors are the colors from red-purple to yellow on the color wheel. These colors affect us psychologically by providing a feeling of warmth and excitement. Visually, these colors appear to project forward. They impart a strong feeling.

Cool colors range from purple to yellow-green on the color wheel. Cool colors feel serene, appear to recede in space, and have a general psychological association with calm.

The fact that warm colors are visually stronger and cool colors more subdued is important as you begin to combine colors. When you use equal amounts of each, the warmer colors are more noticeable. A piece of a design that is yellow will *visually* take up as much space as three or four blue pieces.

To complicate matters, all warm colors can be tempered by mixing in a moderate amount of a cool color, resulting in a less strident version of the color, such as the difference between a blue-based red lipstick and a warm red one. Cool colors can be tempered by adding a little of a warm color, giving the colors a little more heft, such as grass green versus forest green.

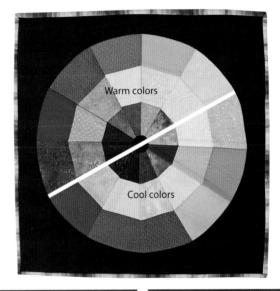

Color temperature: cool red on left, warm red on right

Neutral Colors

Black, white, and gray, colors that are neither warm nor cool, are called *neutral colors*. Keep in mind that many grays have non-neutral colors mixed in—these are *not* neutral. In a palette of warm colors, brown and shades of brown can be used as neutrals as well, offering tones that do not compete with the more vibrant colors.

Color Harmonies: Tried-and-True Color Combinations

There is a general consensus that specific combinations of colors produce harmonious results and color schemes that are aesthetically pleasing.

Monochromatic

A monochromatic color scheme is based on varying values of a particular color. Pale pink with burgundy is an example of a monochromatic color scheme, as is deep teal combined with light turquoise.

Cutting Edge—embroidery designs by author

Crystal Treasures—embroidery designs by author

Multiple shades of gold provide a subdued yet elegant effect.

Tone on tone is certainly monochromatic. This blouse is subtle but beautiful.

Shades of blue showcase a monochromatic tunic.

Celebrations—embroidery designs by author

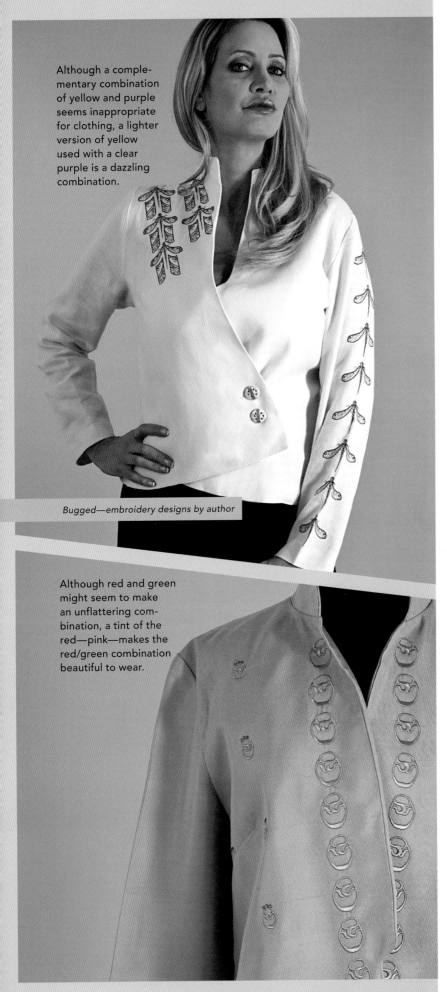

Although a complementary combination of yellow and purple seems inappropriate for clothing, a lighter version of yellow used with a clear purple is a dazzling combination.

Bugged—embroidery designs by author

Although red and green might seem to make an unflattering combination, a tint of the red—pink—makes the red/green combination beautiful to wear.

Complementary

The complementary color scheme uses colors on opposite sides of the color wheel. The most commonly cited complementary relationship is red and green. At first glance, it seems that this combination is not appropriate for clothing other than during the holiday season. However, if you take advantage of the entire wedge of each color, the red/green complementary color scheme is quite stunning. Use tinted red—pink—along with an emerald green to produce a spectacular look.

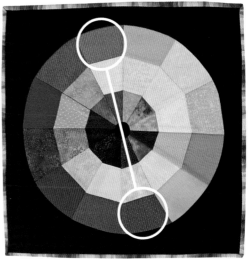

Complementary colors

Split Complementary

The split complementary combination consists of a color and the two colors next to its complement, such as red with yellow-green and turquoise, or blue with orange-yellow and red-orange. The initial reaction to these combinations is that they are not appropriate for clothing. However, move your choices to different rings on the color wheel for charming color combinations.

Split complementary

Analogous Harmony

The analogous color scheme—one of the simplest color combinations—uses three to five colors that are next to each other on the color wheel. Use combinations from the same ring, or add variety and depth by using selections from more than one ring of the color wheel.

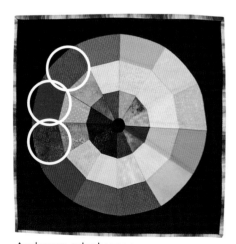

Analogous color harmony

Purple is across the color wheel from yellow, which is bounded by yellow-green and yellow-orange, creating a classic split complementary color combination. To avoid visions of clown clothes, move to the shade ring of the color wheel. This vest uses a deep yellow-green; a deep purple, which appears almost brown; and a deep yellow-orange, also known as orange-brown.

Light & Lacy—embroidery design by author

Peach, golden yellow, and green are also neighbors on the color wheel (analogous colors).

Cutting Edge—embroidery designs by author

Double Complementary

Use two pairs of complementary colors for a double-complementary combination, also known as the *tetrad* (four-color) color combination. Use colors close to each other, or use two pairs farther apart on the color wheel for more contrast.

Though challenging, the double-complementary color scheme can be aesthetic with the judicious use of more and less saturated colors.

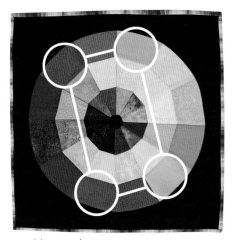

Double complementary

Triad

A combination of three colors equidistant on the color wheel is a *triad* combination. The most recognizable triad uses the three primary colors: red, yellow, and blue. The secondary colors also make up a triad: orange, purple, and green. There are also triads of the tertiary colors.

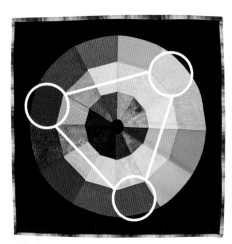

Triad

Putting It All Together in Wearable Art

It seems that any possible pleasing combination of colors is covered in these basic color harmonies. Choose any sampling of colors from the color wheel and it is probable that the choice is one of the harmonies listed. Although this idea seems to make color choices simple, experience tells us otherwise. Wearable art projects are especially challenging.

Use the following variations on the basic color harmonies to create beautiful wearable art.

Vary the Values

The complementary combination of orange and blue sounds inappropriate for clothing. Yet one of the color combinations currently popular consists of brown—a shade of orange—combined with a medium blue, creating a different effect than one would get by using the vibrant cousins of these colors.

Cutting Edge—embroidery designs by author

Brown, a shade of orange, is combined with blue for a striking addition on the leg of these pants.

Vary the Saturation Level

Another way to modify the color combinations is to vary the saturation level. Using desaturated colors almost always produces a pleasing combination, even when using different tints and shades.

Limit Choices to a Single Ring in the Color Wheel

Feeling overwhelmed? Conquer the challenge of the tetrad or double-complementary harmony by limiting your color choices to a single ring in the color wheel. The tetrad harmony of yellow, green, violet, and red is not, initially, an appealing combination. However, using taupe, light green, pale amethyst, and salmon provides stellar results. Choosing a more saturated ring works as well. Pale blues, greens, pinks, and creams are stunning components for a wearable art masterpiece.

Temper Colors with a Generous Amount of a Neutral Color

Many color combinations that look graceless on their own are beautiful when placed against a neutral background. Remember that colors such as brown, cream, taupe, and beige can be used as a background for the same results.

The soft, desaturated colors in this silk blouse blend for an elegant look

Crested Beaut—embroidery designs by author

This very bright blouse uses the suggestion of limiting choices to a single ring in the color wheel. The green, pink, and yellow are bright, bright, bright!

Light & Lacy—embroidery designs by author

Deco Delights (retired set)— embroidery designs by author

This sweet top uses two of the suggestions listed here. First, the colors are limited to a single ring in the color wheel, the tint ring. Then the colors are separated by the generous use of beige, which serves as a neutral.

Crested Beaut—embroidery designs by author

The combination of mango, orange-red, and red-orange is garish when shown in its most vivid state. Desaturate these colors for a wonderful combination.

The white background gives the eye a place to rest between the bold colors on this vest.

Bead Dazzled—embroidery designs by author

NOTE *Separating colors with a neutral line, or stitching designs with space between them on a neutral background, is a great peacemaker. It's similar to the theory that good fences make good neighbors. Give the colors space and they can live in harmony.*

Crested Beaut—embroidery designs by author

The two designs shown above are stitched with the exact same colors of thread. The stitch-outs appear different because of their background fabrics.

Context

A color's appearance depends on its surroundings. Threads that look yellow-green on the spool, or when sewn on white, appear to be cream-colored when placed on a bright lime green. Bright colors look brighter against a black background than they do against a neutral beige. To ensure that the finished project fulfills the design vision without surprises, audition the colors on the intended background.

Mood

Color is the design property that most impacts mood. Tints create a sweet, innocent feeling. Vivid primaries feel childlike and exuberant. Blacks and dark colors are associated with a somber mood. Combinations of colors can also evoke a particular feeling: The high contrast of black and white creates drama, while blues and greens of the same value remind us of serene, natural scenes.

Garment-Specific Color Concepts

Appropriately used color enhances the wearable art creation *and* the wearer— an important component of a beautiful, wearable, and flattering garment. Many of the color combinations that work for other artistic media detract from a garment.

Although color is an important design element for any artistic medium, the garment sewist has specific color concepts to incorporate into his or her piece. Color combinations that elevate other forms of art can actually detract from the overall appearance of a garment. With easily learned modifications, the basic color concepts can be used appropriately in wearable art creations.

Contrast

Choosing an appropriate amount of contrast for the wearer can make or break a garment. For women with a large amount of contrast in their personal coloring, the garment requires high contrast as well. Elizabeth Taylor, with her milky skin and beautiful dark hair, looked better in black and white than in creamy yellows and greens. Jennifer Aniston, with her subtle coloring of light brown hair, pale eyes, and tawny skin, would be overwhelmed in black and white clothing.

The Color Conspiracy

Have you ever noticed how stores all seem to have found the same vat of dye for their clothing lines? One year, everyone is wearing bright and vivid colors. A couple of years later you won't find a clear primary anywhere on the racks. Another year, all the colors are those saturated, rich colors with a predominant trend toward watermelon. I always wondered how the designers instinctively knew what colors were a particular year's "in" colors. Now I know: There's actually a cheat sheet they can access.

Colors follow trends as much as any other part of fashion. While it appears that the designers just happen to be attracted to a particular color range at a particular time, there is a yearly master color plan created by a consortium of designers. It makes sense to know what's in and decide whether or not to join the crowd. And if you have a real preference for one color family or another, you might want to stock up on fabric during the years when your color preference is in vogue.

We love to think that we make classic clothes that will last forever. Unfortunately, the reality of fashion makes that impossible. If you wear clothes that are old, even the ones you thought were classic at the time of purchase, you look odd. Last week at the mall, I saw a woman wearing a "classic" blazer with shoulder pads a linebacker would envy. Despite the classic style, it looked wrong. Colors go in and out of style as well. The color fashion don'ts might not be as obvious as huge shoulder pads, but when you see someone wearing a wine color in a year when everyone else is wearing pistachio, she looks off-kilter.

As Usual, I Learned the Hard Way

I used to think that the whole color/season thing was kind of a scam. I would blithely go about my business wearing any color that struck my fancy. That ended years ago with an eye-opening photo shoot for my website. The shoot consisted of photos of six or seven jackets. I put on piece after piece and pranced around in front of the camera.

When we browsed the pictures, I loved them. The pictures looked great (or as great as any picture of a 50-something-year-old woman who doesn't exactly have a model's body can look). Well, all the pictures looked great, except one—the picture of me wearing a short gray top. The top looked good, perky and sweet, with a moderate amount of embroidery. Unfortunately, I looked like a victim of avian flu. Of course, the first thing I did was blame the photographer (my husband). But it wasn't anything he had done. It was the color of the top. With my coloring, gray clothes mean a gray complexion. A seasonal color proponent was born.

Flattering Colors

The idea of flattering colors gained prominence in the 1970s with the simultaneous publication of a number of books, each of which proposed a color system based on the four seasons of the year. In these books, each season represents a group of colors that flatter people with a particular combination of skin, hair, and eye color. Industries developed around these color systems, including color consultants and lines of makeup.

Fortunately, proponents of the season rules do not have to be limited to their season's colors. By using the flattering colors close to the face, where the impact of a bad color choice shows the most, a designer can introduce other colors into a garment and still allow the wearer to look his or her best. Another method of introducing colors that have the potential to be unflattering is to use small amounts of the less acceptable color.

> **tip** Color should be used to flatter the wearer, since the wearer is always more important than the garment.

The Principles of Design

As anyone who has ever made a garment that just didn't work knows, the act of creating wearable art is more than just throwing assorted elements of line, motif, plane, texture, and pattern on fabric. While these are the building blocks of design, the choice of elements and how they are arranged separate the mundane from the spectacular.

Luckily there is help—concepts to guide us in choosing which elements to use and how and where to place them. These principles of design provide directions for organizing our elements, the building blocks of design.

When the principles of design are appropriately used, the result is a well-designed piece. Although not every principle is used in every piece, the well-designed piece suggests energy, grace, balance, proportion, and rhythm. The parts are harmonious, with the judicious use of repetition among the elements. Appropriate application of these principles determines the effectiveness of the work.

The principles are interconnected and sometimes overlapping. Understanding the principles allows you, as an artist, to spread your wings, knowing which principles to use and which to deliberately exclude. The principles of design give structure. When they feel confining, it's time to abandon them. By understanding them, you'll know when you can effectively abandon and break them.

Repetition

One way to create a visually cohesive piece is to use an element multiple times to provide visual continuity. The repetition can be exact, using the same element multiple times, or it can be a suggested repetition, using similar or slightly altered versions of an element.

Repetition without variation can be either soothing and regular, or boring. Using the same element with variations increases interest. The elements can vary in several ways:

Scale—varying the size of occurrences of an element

Direction—varying the rotation or orientation of an element

Color—varying the hue, shade, or tint of an element

Similarity—using similar but not exact replicas of a motif

Fill—using the same outline with different interiors; repeating one unifying shape but varying the filled-in portion

Outline—using the same content inside different outlines; for example, a circle, a square, and a triangle all filled with the same pattern

The Box

You cannot deliberately work outside the box if you don't know what the box is.

The Goal Is the Thing

The good part about the design principles is that they are guidelines, not hard-and-fast rules. The bad part about the principles is that they are guidelines. There is no one correct way to apply each of the design principles. It's up to us, as artists, to choose what works and what doesn't.

Most graphic design classes begin with "goal" as an important concept. What are you trying to accomplish? Do you need to capture someone's attention, build a mood, motivate a purchase? As a wearable art maker, I have the same goal for all my work: to produce beautiful pieces that are flattering to the wearer. My goal is unchanging and nonnegotiable. Because of this, I don't include focus, center of interest, or goal in the principles of design for wearable art.

The formal alignment of the half-circle motifs in a very structured, symmetrical placement is balanced by the variations within the outlines. Each motif differs in its "innards," providing variety and charm.

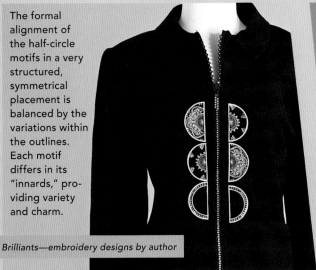

Brilliants—embroidery designs by author

Lines of designs and lines of piping work together to draw the eye up and down. The regularity of the lines could be boring if it weren't for the complexity of the designs. The piping keeps the massive embroidery looking tidy; the repetition of the design creates harmony.

Cutting Edge—embroidery designs by author

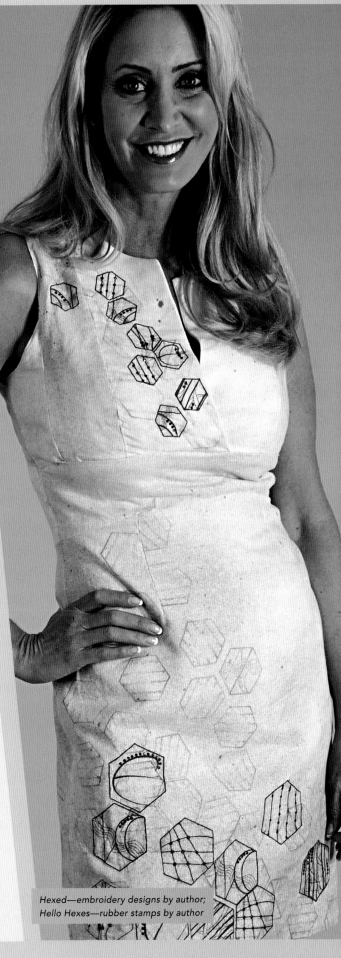

This dress is a study in repetition with variation. The hexagons are used in multiple sizes, multiple colors, and even different media— stamped and embroidered.

This overblouse repeats a single design in multiple colors.

Summer Boxes (retired set)— embroidery designs by author

Hexed—embroidery designs by author; Hello Hexes—rubber stamps by author

Rhythm

Repeating elements in a regular manner with defined spacing creates rhythm. Different kinds of rhythm evoke different feelings. Rhythm can bring a sense of movement, order, predictability, or drama.

Pattern is often rhythmic, as are stripes. If the repeated motif varies in size (scale), the repetition can create depth and involve the viewer. On the other hand, overuse of repetition can be boring.

Balance

In a visually balanced piece, no section feels heavier or more important than any other section. A well-balanced piece feels grounded and comfortable. A painter might choose to create a purposefully unbalanced piece to make the viewer uncomfortable. In wearable art, where the goal is specifically beauty and wearability, balance is a desirable attribute.

No matter what your style prefer-ence, balance is a consideration. Regardless of whether you lean toward grunge, Chanel, steampunk, or retro, balance is a factor. Your goal might be to present something unexpected, but the beauty can still be evident.

Balance can be achieved through symmetrical or asymmetrical design.

Symmetry

Symmetry is balance in which each side of the piece repeats or mirrors the other. Symmetry gives the feeling of calm, tranquility, and significance.

Crown Jewels—embroidery designs by author

Adornments—embroidery designs by author

This jacket illustrates actual symmetry. Horizontally, the black motifs are exactly the same on each side of the jacket.

The regular pattern creates a visual treat on this top.

Mirror images of a single design create a beautiful symmetrical design and add depth to a simple jacket with beautiful lines.

Whimsey—embroidery designs by author

Dragon's Treasure Chest— embroidery designs by author

The stripes are repetitious, as are the elements within the stripes, creating a comfortable yet interesting look and rhythm.

Asymmetry

Asymmetry, also known as informal balance, is a form of virtual balance. The parts, while not exact replicas or mirror images of each other, appear to have equal presence or weight. Asymmetry creates a feeling of excitement, curiosity, or even anxiety.

Asymmetrical balance can be achieved through the placement of elements. Items placed higher on the figure carry more weight than those placed lower. It can also be achieved by using a large number of small objects on one section and a smaller number of larger objects on another.

Using Color to Create Balance

Certain colors, generally brighter colors and warmer ones, carry more weight than others, usually the less saturated and cooler colors.

Cadeau—embroidery designs by author

Hexed—embroidery designs by author

The small number of large designs balances the larger number of small designs in this asymmetrical design. Notice how the line of deep blue (created with fabric strips) helps organize the designs.

Zoo Bits—embroidery designs by author

The large number of small, regularly placed elephants carries as much visual weight as the smaller number of large elephants, creating asymmetrical balance.

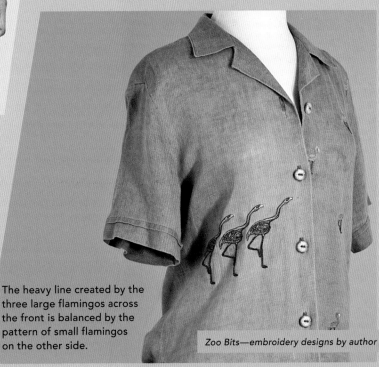

In another approach to asymmetrical design, the sleeves of this jacket are constructed from a textured fabric with a woven stripe, to balance the heavily embroidered fronts.

The heavy line created by the three large flamingos across the front is balanced by the pattern of small flamingos on the other side.

Zoo Bits—embroidery designs by author

Proportion

Proportion refers to the size of one object as it relates to another. In architecture, if the goal is to design a grandiose building, the architect chooses high ceilings to dwarf the individual. In painting, an unusual proportion can initiate thought or bring a feeling of discord; our senses are perplexed when a garage towers over a house or a Clydesdale horse pulls a tiny cart. Incorrect proportion is shocking and thought provoking.

Because the wearable art artist's goal is more specific, to create beauty and flatter the wearer, the use of proportion is more constrained. The goal is a harmonious relationship between the elements within the garment and a pleasing relationship of the garment to the wearer.

Overall Size of the Garment on the Wearer

In garment sewing, it is important that the garment be appropriately sized for both ease (closeness to the body) and overall size in relation to the size of the wearer. The criteria for correct proportion in these two areas are, first of all, what is pleasing to the eye and, second, what is currently fashionable.

In the late 1980s, one style was large, loose tops that reached mid-thigh or below. Twenty years later, the bottom edge of an overblouse stopped at the high hip. Clothes that do not meet whatever current fashion dictates look dated and out of place.

As for proportion in relation to the wearer, small women can be overwhelmed by large, flowing caftans, and large women look silly wearing small garments.

Fit

Another component of proportion in garment sewing is ease, the amount of space between the garment and the body. Ease, like length, is dependent on style. Even the most classically styled suit jacket from the 1990s feels dated today. During the 90s, voluminous clothes were in vogue, while at the arrival of the twenty-first century smaller jackets looked appropriate. The eye becomes accustomed to seeing clothes relate to the body in a certain manner.

Proportion in the Pattern of the Fabric

In wearable art, the relationships of the decorative elements to each other and to the overall garment offer opportunities for a good use of proportion.

To prevent dissonance, decorative elements such as embellishments, embroidered motifs, and beadwork should be sized appropriately when compared with the size of the overall garment, the other decorative elements, and the wearer. A few small dots will look lost on a large overblouse. Making the dots larger or adding more of them can solve the proportion challenge.

Movement

In art, movement—using elements arranged to lead the eye around the piece—is a desirable attribute. Movement creates visual interest and excitement.

Guiding the Eye

Placement of decorative elements can guide the eye, creating a visual flow around the finished project. In clothing design, movement can also enhance the wearer's attractiveness. For example, guiding the eye up and down slims the appearance of the wearer.

Actual Movement

In wearable art, the artist can use actual movement to stimulate the eye. The flow of the fabric as the wearer moves is a way to add beauty and tone to your piece. In that way, the wearable art artist works in four dimensions, not just the two of a painter or the three of a sculptor. Your fabric moves as the wearer moves.

Movement on the Runway

If you need more convincing that fabric movement is an important design factor, visit one of the runway shows' sites on the Internet (such as miami.mbfashionweek.com). Choose a designer whose work features loose, flowy garments. Browse the runway photos and then watch the video. You will see that the movement of the fabric is a very real part of the design.

Though the lines in these designs on the front and the sleeves are made up of multiple elements, they draw the eye up and down.

Zelda—embroidery designs by author

Unity and Harmony

Unity in design is hard to define. It is something that is noted with a glimpse—the sense that all parts of a finished work look like they belong together and function in a coherent manner to create one overall effect.

Although it is related to the principle of repetition (page 30), unity is far broader in scope. It means that no part of the piece is discordant. No single entity or section stands out glaringly or is out of proportion.

As mentioned, unity can be created by using repetition. Sometimes the repeated element can be a variant of the original—changed in size or color. Or one element can suggest another element without being the same at all. For examples of unity in garments, see page 38.

The Final Check

One of the most important steps in my design process is the final check at the completion of every project. Does every element look like it belongs? Does anything stand out as incongruous? Is anything out of place? Is there a lack of harmony between the elements? Tim Gunn of *Project Runway* fame calls this "editing." Whatever you call it, be sure you do it. One part may be beautiful and unique, but if it doesn't fit with the overall project, it will stick out as unprofessional. Stepping back from the piece and making sure the whole looks right—harmonious and unified—is probably the most important step.

Test—Not a Four-Letter Word

Some people can visualize a finished piece and start to work. It's a little harder for me. I visualize with no problem. It's just that when I put my visualization into practice it doesn't always give me the result I expect. My way around this is to test my visions. Some make up exactly as I expect, some work in part, and a few have to be discarded. Throughout this book I explain what and how I test; look for the icons.

> **tip** The principles of design offer a blueprint for a successful way to use the available elements. Study the principles and search for them in everything you see—in artwork, interior design, nature, and especially your own work.

Unity through placement The placement of elements can help unify a piece. For example, the dragonflies on this piece draw the eye up and down, unifying the discordant colors.

Although unity is important, pieces can be too unified. Not enough unity is chaotic and disturbing; too much is boring.

Bugged—embroidery designs by author

Unity through separation This jacket is unified with the addition of the lines. The lines separate the disparate colors so it is not noticeable that the colors in the various sections would clash if placed side by side.

Crested Beaut—embroidery designs by author

Perfecting Your Craft—
Stitching Perfect Designs

While my sewing room may look like a tornado blew through, close examination of my work leaves the viewer with the opposite impression. Because I believe that poor craftsmanship distracts from the beauty of a piece, I work hard to create well-constructed, meticulously fashioned garments. My biggest nightmare is that a new creation will elicit the dreaded "tsk-tsk" from someone examining my work.

In my constant quest for perfection (or, at least, less glaring mistakes), I've streamlined the machine embroidery process, developed tricks, uncovered shortcuts, and identified possible pitfalls and devised ways to avoid them.

My first rule for the pursuit of excellence is to use appropriate, good-quality tools.

39

Embroidery Tools

Although the use of good tools does not guarantee high-quality results in an embroidery project, the use of the wrong, or a poor-quality, tool usually produces less-than-desirable results. Understanding how to match the appropriate thread, stabilizers, machine needles, and embroidery designs to your fabric and your goals is a prerequisite for a well-crafted result. The right tools simplify the embroidery process.

Needles

From the machine embroiderer's point of view, there are three things to consider in choosing a sewing machine needle: the needle point, the thickness of the needle (shaft size), and the size and shape of the eye. Although not a factor in the quality of the stitch, a needle's metal composition affects how long it will last, so it should also be taken into account. The needle types that you see in the store (or online) are a combination of different needle points and different sizes of the eye and shaft.

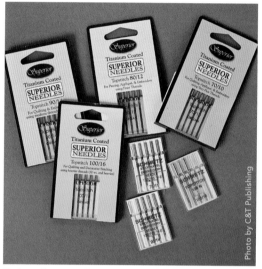

Embroidery needles

COMMON NEEDLE TYPES

	Point	Eye size	Needle sizes
Universal	Between sharp and dull	Small	60/8 to 120/19
Microtex/sharp	Sharp	Small	60/8 to 90/14
Ballpoint/stretch	Dull	Small	70/10 to 100/16
Jeans/denim	Between sharp and dull	Small	70/10 to 110/18
Topstitch	Sharp	Large	70/10 to 100/16
Embroidery	Between sharp and dull	Large	65/9 to 125/20
Metallic	Sharp	Extra large	70/10 to 90/14

Read on for a more complete explanation and recommendations.

Needle Point

Sewing machine needles are available with a choice of points. The most commonly available point types are microtex/sharp, ballpoint/stretch, and universal.

Microtex/sharp point

Ballpoint/stretch point

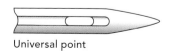

Universal point

Microtex/Sharp

The sharp point is, as the name suggests, sharp. It's designed to go between the threads in a woven fabric. It has a deeper scarf (slot in the side) than other needles to carry thread past the tightly woven fabric. The microtex needle is usually slim, since it is designed for tightly woven, lightweight fabrics. Denim (jeans) needles can be heavier. Topstitch needles also have a sharp point.

Ballpoint/Stretch

The ballpoint and stretch needles sport dull tips to slip between loops of knit fabric without cutting threads. The stretch needle has a deeper scarf to reduce stitch skipping. At this time, some sewists are saying that a stretch needle isn't necessary because you can use a sharp needle for everything. Try a sharp and a stretch needle on your next knit construction project and see which gives you a better result.

Universal

The universal needle point, which has been the most popular needle for many years, is losing its appeal. In theory, the universal needle is halfway between a sharp and a stretch needle, so it can be used on knits or wovens. However, the universal needle is not actually sharp enough for finely woven fabrics or dull enough to slip through the threads in knits without causing snags. Use it on silk dupioni and watch the needle draw up the threads, leaving runs. With many knits, you'll have similar results.

Needle Size

Needles come in an assortment of sizes ranging from 60/8 to 125/20. The large number is the diameter of the main part of the needle, called the *blade*. This number represents hundredths of a millimeter; for example, a size 70 needle is .70mm in diameter. The small number in the sizing is an arbitrary number consistently used by American manufacturers.

Choose the needle size according to the fabric thickness and strength, as well as the thickness of the thread. Find a needle slim enough to pierce the fabric without leaving a noticeable hole and strong enough not to break when used.

The Search for the Perfect Needle

A few years ago I, along with 29 other fiber artists, had the pleasure of attending Bernina Camp, a four-day visit to Bernina headquarters. Our Bernina hosts gave us tours of the facilities, introduced us to Bernina executives, and treated us to classes using their best machines. One of the seminars was led by the head of the technical team. This brilliant man knew all about the idiosyncrasies of sewing machines and the potential problems we might encounter. How did he choose to use his allotted hour? We had a clue when he walked into the room with a foot-and-a-half-tall sewing machine needle. He spent the entire time telling us how important the sewing machine needle is for perfect stitching. (We never did get to see the sewing machine that the needle came from.)

After my visit to Bernina Camp, I paid much more attention to machine needles. Once I started looking, I discovered that there were a lot of places where my beautiful, wonderful silk fabrics had little runs from needles with rounded points. I decided to use only sharps on my woven fabrics. Not one to do anything halfway, I bought a box of 100 sharp needles and started using them. I immediately saw a difference with fewer pulled threads. No more little runs in my silks!

Unfortunately, I started to experience other problems: My stitch-outs looked dull, without the usual gorgeous sheen. My machine also seemed to have more problems with lint, thread shredding around the eye of the needle, and thread breakage. What was happening?

It took a while to figure it out, but I realized that the problem was the new needles—the embroidery thread rubbed against the needle because the eye was too small. After I figured that out, I had a new quest—the search for a sharp embroidery needle.

I didn't find a sharp embroidery needle, but I found something that works as well: a topstitch needle from Superior Threads. I was so impressed that I started stocking these needles for my business.

The following are suggestions for choosing the correct needle for any given fabric.

NEEDLE CHOICE BY FABRIC

Fabric	Needle size/type
Woven fabrics	
Lightweight fabrics such as batiste, chiffon, crepe de chine, georgette, voile, broadcloth, challis, crepe, lawn, and handkerchief linen	65/9 embroidery or 70/10 topstitch
Medium-weight fabrics such as quilting-weight cotton, broadcloth, silk shantung or dupioni, and muslin	70/10 or 80/12 topstitch
Heavier fabrics such as toweling, upholstery fabric, duck, coating, or jeans-weight denim	90/14 or larger topstitch
Knit fabrics	
Light- to medium-weight jersey knits or spandex swimwear	75/11 or 80/12 embroidery
Sweatshirt fabric or double-knit polyester	90/14 embroidery

Needle Eye

Needles used for machine embroidery require a larger eye than those used for other sewing. Machine embroidery thread is thicker than and, in the case of rayon thread, not as strong as standard sewing thread. Because it runs at higher speeds and performs longer continuous stitching than a standard sewing machine, the embroidery machine and a small-eyed needle are not a good pair. Use needles with eyes big enough for the thread to pass through without shredding.

Most embroidery needles have a large eye but do not have a sharp point. Another option is to use a topstitch needle, which has both a large eye and a sharp point.

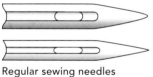

Regular sewing needles

Topstitch or embroidery
sewing needles

Not Universal

It took me years to understand what caused those tiny pulls in my fine silks and that a universal needle is not really "universal." I used to accept the little runs at the edges of my embroidery designs; now I know that using a good sharp needle, instead of a universal, leaves my fabric intact. I recommend that you stock both topstitch needles for woven fabric and embroidery needles for knits and get rid of your universal needles.

Needle Life

Machine needles have a limited life span. Often a microscope will show wear on the point of the needle even when it looks sharp to the naked eye. There is no exact formula to determine when a needle should be changed. Stitching on polyester fabrics dulls a needle faster than stitching through a natural fabric. Tightly woven fabrics give more resistance, wearing the needle more quickly than looser weaves. One suggestion is to change the needle after every eight hours of stitching. When you stitch intensive projects, change the needle before the beginning of a new project. When your embroidery designs are particularly dense, change the needle even more often.

Metallic Needles

Metallic thread can give you a headache, but if you choose to use it, use a metallic needle. It has an extra-large eye that is in some brands coated with Teflon to ease the passage of the delicate thread through the metal eye.

In addition to how long a needle has been in use, there are a number of signs that indicate you need to change the needle:

- Loops on the surface of the stitched design
- Odd popping sounds made by the machine every time the needle hits the fabric
- Thread nests

When in doubt, change the needle.

tip Some needles are available with a titanium coating that extends the needle life. They are more expensive, but they do last longer.

Thread

Thread is the public face of machine embroidery. The rich colors and beautiful sheen are important components of the beauty of the finished piece.

Photo by C&T Publishing

Embroidery thread

Thread Weight

In the numbering system for thread weight, the higher the number, the finer the thread. The very fine, lightweight thread used in heirloom sewing is 60-weight. Most thread used for garment construction is 50-weight, a little heavier than the heirloom thread. The denser thread used for covering space with machine embroidery is 40-weight, a much thicker thread. When you are shopping for thread, you will see on the spool either the weight or the Gunze Count (the weight of the threads used to make the plies / the number of plies used to make the thread); the more plies, the heavier the thread, so given the same weight plies, a three-ply thread is thicker than a two-ply thread.

More than 50, Less than a Million

In some of my classes I open with the question, "Who in here has more than ten spools of embroidery thread?" It's like I'm David Letterman. The room rocks with laughter and every single person raises a hand. "More than twenty?" brings the same response. Face it; we machine embroiderers have huge collections of thread. Unfortunately, some machine embroiderers choose quantity over quality, leading to less-than-perfect machine embroidery.

We spend thousands of dollars on a machine, so why skimp on thread? Would you put substandard gas in your car? Probably not, so don't choose embroidery thread by price and then wonder why the results are poor.

THREAD WEIGHTS

Thread type	Weight	Gunze count	Common use
Light	60-weight	#60/3	Bobbin, appliqué, heirloom sewing
Thin	50-weight	#50/3	Bobbin, appliqué, garment sewing
Regular	40-weight	#40/3	Embroidery and quilting
Upholstery	30-weight	#30/3	Decorative
Heavy	20-weight	#20/3	Decorative

Chart based on "Thread (Yarn)," Wikipedia.org

It's important to use the appropriate weight and type of thread for machine embroidery. Most designs are set up for 40-weight embroidery thread. Sewing with a lighter-weight thread will not cover the space in the way the digitizer designed. Using a heavier thread will give, at best, an overly dense design, and at worst, tangled threads, thread nests, and broken embroidery needles.

Unless the design specifically states something different, choose a 40-weight thread designed for machine embroidery. Regular sewing thread designed for construction will not give good results in an embroidery machine.

 Test stitch samples of your selected designs with the needles and threads you intend to use on your chosen fabric to make sure the designs stitch out as desired.

Fiber Type

Embroidery thread is generally spun from either rayon or polyester. Each has its strengths and weaknesses.

Rayon

Rayon thread has been the standard for machine embroidery for years. It was not until the turn of the twenty-first century that polyester threads were able to compete with rayon in luster and shine. Although rayon thread can be easily snapped in the hands, in the sewing machine its flexibility provides stability in stitching with few breaks. The biggest disadvantage to rayon thread is that it fades when subjected to bleach, so it is not the best choice for towels, napkins, or other items that will be laundered in harsh circumstances.

Polyester

Polyester threads vary in quality. Some polyester threads are as vibrant and shiny as rayon; others, not so much. For example, the polyester machine embroidery thread made by Superior Threads is a trilobal thread. It is manufactured by shooting the chemicals through triangular holes, forming a three-sided thread. The three sides of the thread work in a manner similar to the planes of a crystal, reflecting light to create a beautiful, shiny surface. Other polyester threads are made differently and do not have the same shine.

I Love Shiny Things

Ah, the texture of a beautiful fill stitch, the gloss and grace of satin stitch—machine embroidery can be gorgeous. Most of us think of sheen and rich colors as a part of the embroiderer's craft. To achieve this look, we depend on shiny, glossy thread. My personal preference is rayon thread. It always comes through with a gleaming beauty. I know that some of the polyester threads have a sheen, but I've had experience with polyesters that look good on the spool but stitch out dull. I also worry that the strength of polyester thread must be hard on the tension disks of the sewing machine.

Having said all that, when I embroider towels, swimwear, aprons, or napkins—anything that will be exposed to bleach—I reach for polyester thread.

To add spice to your work, a variety of specialty threads are available, including metallic, holographic, and glow-in-the-dark threads, as well as solar-activated threads that change color when exposed to sunlight. Although these threads can add interest to your work, be aware that some threads, such as metallics, add a challenge when stitching. Your best strategy for working with specialty threads is to have a perfect thread path, including these elements:

- A clean sewing machine that is threaded correctly

- Thread that is on the correct type of spool pin (see Stack-Wound and Cross-Wound, below)

- The appropriate needle for the type and size of thread (pages 42 and 44)

---

tip Consider placing your thread farther from the machine than the standard spool pins allow. Using a thread stand that is farther from the machine gives the thread time to straighten and unkink, which is crucial for metallics but can also help with other threads.

All Wound Up

In addition to using the correct thread type and weight, it's important to know how the thread is wound on the spool. Stack-wound thread is in an even spiral on the spool, while cross-wound thread crosses over itself diagonally on the spool.

Stack-Wound

Stack-wound thread works best with the thread unwinding straight from the side of the spool and the spool spinning freely as it unwinds. If the spool is on a vertical thread pin, set the thread path so that the spool can spin as it releases thread. Stack-wound thread can be used with a horizontal thread pin if the thread path travels upward, allowing the spool to spin. (The manufacturers of stack-wound thread may suggest that you put a thread net over the spool to keep the thread from reeling off in an uncontrolled manner.)

Cross-Wound

Cross-wound thread is generally easier to work with than stack-wound thread. Manufacturers choose to cross-wind their thread so it leaves the spool with even tension. Most of the better threads are wound in a cross-wise pattern. This design causes the exiting thread to travel up and down the spool or cone, reducing stress on the thread. You can use almost any delivery system with cross-wound thread as long as the thread unwinds by traveling over the top of the spool.

Stack-wound thread

Cross-wound thread

Only the Best

Which embroidery threads work best seems to be a guess. I've seen two identical machines threaded with two identical spools of thread of the same brand. The first machine will work great, yet the other chews the thread into shreds. Changing the thread to a different brand sets the errant machine humming.

To keep us on our toes, the newest machines on the market seem to be even more finicky than the older ones.

A few months ago, I took advantage of a friend's offer to use her new big-hoop machine. Not only did she offer me the use of her machine, but she also offered me access to her copious collection of embroidery threads. She pointed at one section and said, "That brand of thread has lovely colors but it's temperamental." She pulled out a box from another shelf and said, "This is Isacord. I haven't used it in this machine yet, but it is always consistent in my other machines."

You can probably guess where this is heading. For most of the stitching, I used my own Robison-Anton threads with perfect results. I was close to the end of the design when I discovered that I had left a critical color at home. I opened the cabinets to raid my friend's stash. First I tried a spool from the brand she had labeled temperamental. Temperamental was an understatement! I expected some thread shredding and some breaks, but no, it was worse than that. My beautiful embroidery was dotted with loops! After some quality time with my stitch ripper, I tried again. This time I used the Isacord she had labeled tried and true. I'll be darned—the Isacord gave me loops, too. I went back to my Robison-Anton thread.

I'm not saying that Robison-Anton is the only thread you should use; in fact, your machine might work well with many different brands. I am just saying I have had consistent results from it on a wide variety of machine brands. When I teach embroidery classes, I have never seen the Robison-Anton thread mess up on any machine.

Choosing Embroidery Thread

On the spool, all embroidery threads look spectacular. It is not until the actual stitching that the variation in quality shows. When choosing embroidery thread, first make sure a thread is really designed to be embroidery thread. Next, decide whether you want polyester or rayon. Of course, the quality of the thread is important, too.

 The last, and possibly most important, decision in choosing thread is choosing the brand. Although it is tempting to shop by price, make sure the thread you take home works well with your machine. Before investing in a large number of spools of a particular brand, make sure you test. Nothing is more irritating than to have a large collection of thread of a brand that doesn't agree with your machine. You don't want your machine rebelling by shredding thread or producing loops and uneven stitches.

Bobbin Thread

Consider strength, weight, and color when choosing bobbin thread for embroidery. The bobbin thread needs to be strong enough to stand up to the high speed of an embroidery machine. It should be lightweight to facilitate the appropriate ratio between thread on the front and thread on the back of the stitch-out—machine embroidery looks best when much of the top thread is pulled to the back of the fabric; no bobbin thread should show on the front. Although bobbin thread comes in a variety of colors, white and black are the most popular. If your machine works with prewound bobbins, they're a good option because they generally hold more thread than a bobbin you wind yourself.

Bobbin thread

Color Blind

A while back, my favorite embroidery conspirator asked if I wanted to split two boxes of prewound bobbins, one black and one white. While I'm a huge proponent of prewound bobbins, I had never used black bobbins. Yet it makes sense. I still have no idea why I never thought to use black thread! If you use a dark bobbin thread when embroidering on black or dark fabric, the back of the project will look better.

On a similar note, in a class I was teaching recently, one of the students had a box of bobbins, each wound with a different color of embroidery thread. It seemed that she always used a bobbin thread that matched her embroidery thread. When she didn't, the bobbin thread would show on top. My immediate response was that if your bobbin thread is showing on top, *your machine needs servicing!* Your bobbin thread should never show!

Stabilizers

It's not a secret that when a sewing machine takes a stitch, the stitch pulls the fabric, causing it to contract. When multiple stitches are sewn close together, as they are in machine embroidery, the fabric is pulled in the direction of the stitching, causing puckers. Stabilizer is a piece of fabric or heavy paper, or a chemical compound that has been pressed into a paperlike sheet, that adds strength and holds the fabric firmly, keeping it from puckering or pulling together as the machine stitches.

Poor stabilization This design has the potential to be beautiful, but insufficient stabilization is allowing puckers.

Bugged—embroidery designs by author

Correct stabilization The same design on the same fabric, but with correct stabilization.

Cut-away stabilizer

Stabilizers

Factors to Consider

Although there are a wide variety of stabilizers on the market, it is possible to cover almost every need with four types (pages 50–52). The choice of stabilizer depends on several factors:

- The stability or stretchiness of the base fabric
- The density and quality of the embroidery design
- How much of the stabilizer it is acceptable to leave in
- Whether or not the back of your finished project will show
- How the stabilizer will be removed

Fabric Stability

For a beautiful finished product, the fabric surface needs to remain stable. Slippery, light, or stretchy fabrics require heavy stabilizer. Solid, firm fabrics require little or no stabilizer.

Imagine a rating system for the stability of fabrics, from one to six. Very stable fabrics, such as terry cloth and denim, are rated a six, and stretchy knits are rated a one (unstable). Likewise, stabilizers are rated from the firmest (five) down to none (zero).

To produce a high-quality embroidery stitch-out, the combination of fabric and stabilizer requires total stability equal to a six. Pairing unstable fabric with a firm stabilizer offers sufficient stability for a good stitch-out. Putting a fairly stable fabric with a light stabilizer gives the same results. In the following chart, stabilizer stability plus fabric stability equals total stability level.

STABILITY LEVELS

Stabilizer stability	Fabric stability	Total stability level
Firm stabilizer 5	Stretchy fabric 1	6
Medium stabilizer 3	Stable wool crepe 3	6
No stabilizer 0	Silk organza 6	6

Note: With a very stable fabric, the only reason to use a stabilizer would be if the fabric is so thin (for example, a silk organza) that it slips out of the hoop without the added bulk of a stabilizer.

Density of the Embroidery Design

Every stitch stitched in an embroidery design pulls the fabric; hence, the more stitches, the greater the possibility for pull and its accompanying puckering. The closer the stitches are to each other, the more pull. A design with more fill stitches (rows and rows of stitches next to each other) requires more stabilization than a design consisting of lightly populated run stitches.

Zoo Bits—embroidery designs by author

Fill stitch

On the Table—embroidery designs by author

Run stitch

Quality of the Embroidery Design

Another factor in choosing stabilizer is whether or not the design includes underlay. Underlay is a series of stitches underneath the top layer or visible part of the embroidery design. Underlay supports the embroidery. For fill stitches, the underlay should run perpendicular to the fill, forming a foundation to hold the fabric flat. For satin stitches, the underlay can run either perpendicular to the stitches or in a zigzag pattern. Underlay keeps the fabric from pulling in and creating puckers.

Crested Beaut—embroidery designs by author

Satin stitch

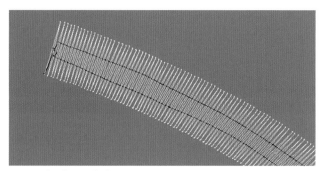

Perpendicular underlay

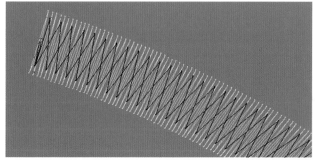

Zigzag underlay

How Much Stabilizer Will Be Left In?

Some stabilizers are completely removed after stitching (wash-away and heat-away), and others are partially removed (tear-away–wash-away). An important decision is how much, if any, stabilizer should be left in the finished project.

Stabilizer keeps fabric unpuckered only for as long as the stabilizer is present. After a stabilizer is removed, the stabilizer no longer provides a foundation for the stitching. Embroidery that stays pucker free after the stabilizer is removed depends on a combination of sufficiently firm fabric, designs that are not too dense, and the appropriate amount of underlay.

Knits and very light or loosely woven fabrics are often too light to support a dense embroidery design. Sometimes poorly digitized designs with insufficient underlay allow too much pull (and therefore puckers) when stabilizer is removed. These fabrics and designs give the best results when stabilizer is left under the embroidery to keep the fabric from collapsing.

I used to say that there are two kinds of people in the world: those who care what the insides of their garments look like and those who don't. For years, I was in the "don't care" camp. When I started doing trunk shows for a living though, hundreds—sometimes thousands—of people were looking at my clothes—the inside as well as the outside. Suddenly, how my clothes looked inside became very important to me.

Now that inside perfection has become a priority, I dislike leaving stabilizer in my garments. Unless I absolutely can't, I remove the stabilizer.

Using a stabilizer that is not designed to be removed can create problems of its own. Stabilizer is usually stiffer than the fashion or surface fabric, changing its hand (amount of drape). Stiff stabilizer can often be seen on the right side of the project, its hard edge shadowing the embroidery design. In addition, the stiff edge can be uncomfortable to wear.

How Will the Stabilizer Be Removed?

The method of removing the stabilizer *must* be appropriate for the fabric. Wash-away stabilizers are for washable fabrics (don't forget to prewash your fabrics). For dry-clean-only silks or wools, choose a heat-away stabilizer.

Some fabrics are so light that any embroidery design, even a design with a good underlay, will overwhelm the fabric once the stabilizer is removed. For these fabrics, choose either a stabilizer that remains in the fabric or one that partially remains.

The Well-Equipped Stabilizer Stash

Four basic stabilizers will cover most of your embroidery needs: wash-away, tear-away–wash-away, cut-away, and heat-away.

Wash-Away Stabilizer

Wash-away, or water-soluble, stabilizers dissolve with cold water. These wonderful stabilizers have the look, feel, and strength of a cut-away, but they easily wash out. Most brands on the market today are made of the same chemicals and therefore wash away at the same rate.

 As with so many embroidery products, testing the stabilizer is an important step. If you plan to use a wash-away stabilizer, test to make sure it will be totally eliminated from your project.

Be aware that wash-away stabilizers must be completely removed before the design is pressed. Pressing the design before removing the stabilizer hardens the stabilizer, changing it so it is no longer water soluble. If the removal is incomplete, ironing can also cause stains on the fabric.

Wash-away stabilizer is a good choice for use with cottons, linens, rayons, and other washable fabrics that can support a finished embroidery design. It also works well if you are planning to wash your silks.

Wash-away stabilizer

Tear-Away–Wash-Away Stabilizer

Tear-away–wash-away stabilizers resemble heavy drawing paper. They offer a great amount of stability for beautiful stitch-outs with little puckering or pulling.

After stitching, remove the majority of the stabilizer by tearing it away from the edges of the design. Then wash the project in the washing machine. The stabilizer will remain under the fill-stitched sections and in some satin-stitched areas.

Choose either a wash-away stabilizer or a tear-away–wash-away stabilizer based on whether or not your design will require some support in the finished project, and on whether or not a little stiffness under the embroidery design is acceptable.

Tear-away–wash-away stabilizer

Heat-Away Stabilizer

A heat-away stabilizer is removed with a hot iron. After the stabilizer is heated, older versions darken, turn dark brown or black, and then transform into ash, which can be brushed away. The newer heat-away stabilizers bubble and then melt totally away, leaving tiny pearls. Heat-aways are perfect in wool or silk projects in which the back of the fabric is exposed.

It's Good and Expensive

I would use a heat-away stabilizer all the time if I weren't so cheap. It's just too expensive! Having said that, I often use heat-aways for silks and wools.

Heat-away stabilizer

The Thick and Thin of It

I have an unjustified dislike of cut-away stabilizers left over from the time when cut-aways were stiff and thick and showed through fabric. Now cut-aways are thin and supple. They're stable yet light enough that their edges aren't visible through even the lightest fabrics.

If you haven't tried them lately, give them a try, especially for embroidering on knits.

A Sticky Subject

The stabilizer shelves in the sewing stores are filled with what feels like an infinite variety of stabilizers. If wash-away, tear-away, sticky, heat-away, and cut-away stabilizers aren't enough, there are variations on each of these: wash-aways that are also sticky, cut-aways of different weights, and so on.

In the old days, when there were fewer stabilizer offerings, my stand against sticky stabilizers shocked many embroiderers. Most people thought that sticky stabilizers were miraculous because they held the fabric in exactly the right place, eased the challenge of hooping, and practically eliminated puckering. I, on the other hand, could see only the downside of the sticky stabilizer. I resented the hours spent picking out tiny pieces of stabilizer from around the stitches, and I hated the gummy residue remaining on the back of a project.

Now sticky stabilizers come in a variety of formats, including a water-soluble sticky stabilizer. This product has the good points of a sticky stabilizer without the evil leftover residue. The only down-side is the cost. I choose to populate the stabilizer section of my sewing room with only four types of stabilizer: wash-away, tear-away–wash-away, cut-away, and heat-away. I find that with a good spray adhesive I don't need anything else.

Cut-Away Stabilizer

A cut-away stabilizer permanently remains in the project to give stability both during and after the stitching. Most knits are best embroidered with a cut-away so that as the garment is worn, the fabric doesn't stretch and pop the embroidery threads. Cut-aways are appropriate for lined projects, where the back of the embroidery doesn't show, or for knits or loosely woven fabrics that require permanent stabilization.

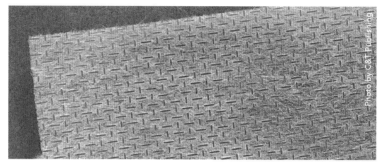

Cut-away stabilizer

Other Stabilizers

Despite the large variety of stabilizers available today, most stabilizing needs can be met with the basic four stabilizers described above. If your fabric needs more stabilization, just use another sheet of the appropriate stabilizer.

Spray Adhesives

Temporary spray adhesives are a great tool for the machine embroiderer. They can be used to stick fabric to the stabilizer to prevent distortion or puckering, a boon for loosely woven or slinky fabrics, especially knits. Temporary spray adhesive is also useful for temporarily adhering appliqué fabric before it is stitched into place.

Use a temporary spray adhesive to attach fabric pieces smaller than your hoop to hooped stabilizer. For example, to stitch a design on a collar or cuff, hoop the stabilizer, spray the piece with adhesive, and then stick it to the stabilizer for stitching.

Another use for temporary spray adhesive is to prevent hoop marks. Some fabrics, like velvets and suedes, will permanently crease in the shape of a hoop. Instead of hooping the fabric, hoop the stabilizer and use temporary spray adhesive to hold the fabric in place.

As with so many of the tools suggested, test any temporary spray adhesive before use.

Temporary spray adhesives

My Favorite Spray Adhesives

I'm a strong proponent of spray adhesives to make embroidering easier. However, I'm picky about my adhesives. I've had adhesives that left sticky messes, others that stained the fabric, and yet others that stuck to my iron. At this time I use only Sulky KK 2000 or Gunold KK 100. There are, supposedly, some technical differences between the two products, but as far as I can tell, the only difference is price, the Gunold being the less expensive but harder to find offering.

As with so many of my recommendations, I don't profess to know everything. It's possible that there are other adhesives out there that work without making more problems than they solve, but I haven't found them.

Scissors

A sharp scissors with a tiny, pointed tip is a useful tool in the embroidery room. A curved tip makes it easier to clip thread ends close to the fabric or to trim excess fabric from the edge of an appliqué before the final stop stitching.

Very Sharp Scissors

I have to make a note here about Kai scissors. I have never found a sharper, more precise scissors. Small, curved Kai scissors clip threads extremely close to the fabric. Here's another item I added to my business because of its high quality.

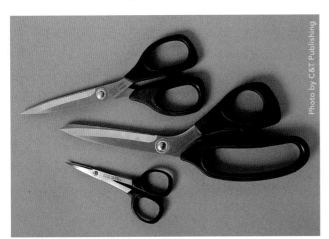

Scissors

Rulers

For good placement and design alignment, it's useful to have a variety of rulers. At a minimum, choose one ruler short enough to fit within the boundaries of your embroidery hoop and another that is 5″–6″ longer than your largest embroidery hoop. Clear rulers with easy-to-read markings work best.

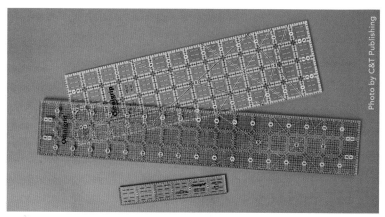

Rulers

Centering Rulers

A third-party vendor, Designs in Machine Embroidery, offers Eileen Roche's Embroidery Tool Kit, which includes a wonderful product: centering rulers. These are adhesive strips to apply to the four sides of the edge of your favorite hoop. The center of each strip is marked with zero; the ruler starts there, and the distances radiate out from the center. The kit also includes other rulers to aid in spacing and placement.

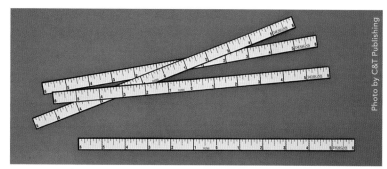

Centering rulers from Designs in Machine Embroidery

Marking Pens

An integral part of the placement process is marking. It's important to be able to draw on your fabric, placing marks that can be completely removed after the embroidery process is finished.

The choice of marking devices depends on your fabric. A water-soluble pen is a good choice when sewing on washable cotton. An air-soluble pen works well for fabric that cannot be treated with water. Some wools can be marked with soap or wax. When pressed, the soap or wax melts into the wool.

In some cases, marking with basting stitches may be your best option.

 You will need to mark for accurate placement. Test to make sure the marks can be removed after stitching.

Marking pens

Marking a Mark

I have a love-hate relationship with marking pens. I use them all the time and couldn't get along without them. Yet they terrify me. I know they sit in my drawer, planning my demise. I'll use a pen one week and it behaves properly, politely disappearing with a light spray of water. The next time I use it, that same pen will make permanent marks that turn brown and stubbornly refuse to leave my project.

 Once more the lesson is test, test, test! Test on fabric similar to the fabric you will use for the actual project.

The Embroidery Machine

When buying an embroidery machine, one of the most important decisions is which dealer to buy from. Choose a dealer who holds classes on the machine's features, how to use the machine, how to care for the machine, and so on. A good dealer will support you and stand behind the machine.

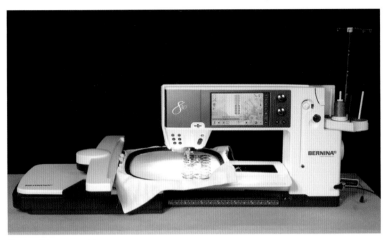

Embroidery machine

Must-Have Features

Must-Have: A Large Hoop

Choose an embroidery machine with the largest hoop your budget will allow. The larger the hoop, the more space you can cover in each hooping. Even if your current style is to sew small designs in small spaces, a machine with a small hoop limits your future choices. A large hoop allows you to combine designs to cover a large space and to purchase a wider variety of designs. The smallest "large" hoop you should consider buying is 5″ × 7″. Bigger than that is even better.

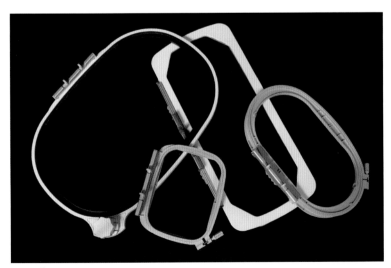

Large hoops

The Number 1 Question

If I had a nickel for every time someone asked me what sewing machine they should buy, I'd have a lot of nickels! As boring as it sounds, my answer is the one you hear from any teacher not affiliated with a particular brand: "Find a dealer you like, and buy what he or she sells." Does it sound like a cop-out? It isn't. Unless you know a lot about sewing and embroidery machines, that's the way to go. Almost all the machines work, and work well. You face a huge learning curve when you're starting out. You will be happier climbing that curve with someone to guide you. So my advice is to find a dealer whose company you really enjoy.

My Must-Haves

Note that it *is* possible to achieve excellent results without the features I consider mandatory—it's just harder. Evaluate for yourself. I do promise that your life as an embroiderer will be easier when you have the features I have listed.

Size Counts

Anyone who says that size doesn't matter hasn't owned an embroidery machine. From my point of view, the larger the embroidery hoop, the better. If I had my way, every machine would come with a hoop the size of a picture window. Right now I'm using a Bernina 830 with a hoop that is 10″ wide and almost 16″ long! Not a picture window, but close.

SINGLE-POSITION HOOP VERSUS MULTI-POSITION HOOP

Some machines offer hoops that look big but require position changes. For these hoops, you attach the hoop at the top position and sew a portion of the design. When the machine signals, you must move the hoop to a different position and stitch more of the design. Some multi-position hoops are more user-friendly than others. For example, the Viking Designer SE's multi-position hoop allows you to load large designs. The sewing machine splits the designs for the multiple positions. With this machine, any design that fits within the hoop's boundaries can be stitched.

Another offering by Viking (the Viking Designer I) requires that the design be split for the multiple positions before it is loaded into the machine. Though less desirable than the functionality of the SE model, this limitation is acceptable to some because a large variety of these pre-split designs are available for purchase. In addition, users comfortable with a computer can use software to split any design before loading it into the machine.

Be aware that some of the machines with multi-position hoops do not split the designs and have very few pre-split designs available to buy. These machines should only be considered by users who enjoy spending time on the computer. How do you know what a machine can do? Ask the machine dealer.

> **tip** A great source of brand-specific information and conversation is online groups, such as those found on Yahoo (groups.yahoo.com).

Must-Have: Easy Design Delivery

Before purchasing an embroidery machine, evaluate the method used to install embroidery designs in the machine for stitching: The simpler the method, the easier the embroidering. Make sure you understand the hardware and software required, and the process. If possible, practice the steps before purchase.

At this time, the most desirable method for delivering designs to the sewing machine is using your computer's file management system to copy a design onto a generic USB stick (see Easy-Peasy Delivery, below), just as you would move or copy any other type of file. (Some embroidery machines can only use machine-specific USB sticks—another hidden expense.) Being limited to the machine manufacturer's software for moving designs onto the machine adds another level of complexity and expense.

Machine-specific memory card

The history of the home embroidery machine explains some of the design delivery options still available today.

The first embroidery machines were designed to use machine-specific memory cards to deliver designs to the machine. These cards require a separate box attached to the computer. The cards are expensive and require expensive, machine-specific software. Though these machines are now rare, a few current versions are still being sold and you can find used machines of this type.

Easy-Peasy Delivery

Even though I'm very comfortable with computers and software, my favorite machines have a simple method for installing designs. I don't have the time to deal with proprietary software or the money to spend on machine-specific USB sticks. I am too busy and too frugal for that.

Machine embroidery became less expensive when the machine manufacturers began using computer data storage options such as floppy disks, CDs, and, later, USB sticks for transferring designs. Some manufacturers allow you to use the computer's own file management system to move the designs from the computer to the disk, CD, or USB stick, lowering the cost even more. Other manufacturers only allow transfers with their software, requiring that you purchase that software.

Even though every manufacturer now has some models of machines that allow design installation without proprietary software, the less user-friendly machines are still marketed. Most of the manufacturers' low-end machines use older technology, as do some of the used machines that are still available. Be aware of the limitations of some of these "bargain" machines.

When choosing a machine, be sure you are comfortable with the steps required to install designs on it. If possible, choose a machine that uses generic USB sticks and will allow you to load designs using your computer's file management system.

If you aren't sure about any of this, ask the dealer as many questions as necessary to be sure you understand the process.

Floppy disks and CDs

USB sticks

Must-Have: Customizing on the Screen

Every machine manufacturer has at least one model with the ability to easily manipulate (customize) the designs on the embroidery machine itself. All of these allow you to load more than one design at a time and then move each of the designs around, arranging them to your taste. Most machines allow the designs to be rotated 90° or 180°; some high-end machines allow rotation 1° at a time.

For those very comfortable using computers, the manipulation in the machine is not as important, but even the most computer-savvy embroiderer will, on occasion, want to add and arrange designs on the sewing machine instead of on the computer.

Must-Have: Positioning Feature

As your embroidery projects increase in sophistication, the skill of positioning a design in an exact location on the fabric becomes more and more important. Perfect hooping requires skill and patience. Using the machine's ability to shift a design allows less precise hooping, a more attainable goal. Although design shifting is a standard feature, the way it is performed is easier with some machine models than with others.

This design placement could use improvement.

A more pleasing arrangement

The method used most often for placing a design in a specific spot begins with marking fabric in the center of the target location. Optimally, after it is marked, the fabric is hooped with the mark centered exactly. When the hoop is placed in the machine, the needle is centered in the hoop, corresponding with the center of the loaded design. If you have not hooped the fabric perfectly, the needle will not be over the center mark on the fabric; instead, it will hover a small distance away. You can use arrows on the machine's screen to shift the center of the design (indicated by the needle) over to the marked center, allowing the design to be stitched in the desired place. (For more information see Hooping, pages 63–66.)

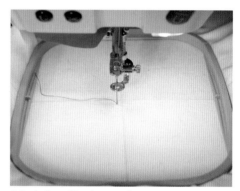

A little bit off—the needle is not exactly over the crosshairs.

Some machines only allow you to shift a design before *any stitching* takes place. A machine that does not allow movement after the first stitch of a design causes extra work.

Desirable Features

The features in the desirable category are not must-haves, but they are definitely nice to have. If you do a lot of embroidery you'll want them as well.

Desirable: Auto-Resume

One of the best innovations in home embroidery machines is the addition of the auto-resume feature. With auto-resume, a machine that is interrupted while stitching will restart exactly where it stopped.

Desirable: Speed

There's a noticeable difference in stitching speed from one machine to the next. No matter how much embroidery you do, faster is better.

Desirable: Color Sort

Loading multiple copies of the same design for a single hooping is a common action in machine embroidery. When you do this, the color changes become inefficient. A common example is to load seven copies of a small flower scattered in a large hoop. To stitch the first flower, you'll stitch the following colors:

Color 1—green for the leaves

Color 2—pink for the flower petals

Color 3—yellow for the center of the first flower

To stitch the second flower, the machine starts all over with the green, and then it repeats the three-color sequence for every flower.

Color sorting eliminates duplicate thread changes by having the machine stitch all the green leaves first. Then you change the thread and stitch all the flower petals. Change the thread again and finish with all the flower centers. Most high-end machines include an option for sorting the colors over multiple designs.

Auto-Resume, My Love!

Inevitably, it happens. Someone trips on a plug, or the power goes out, or you think you're finished but you're not. No matter the cause, when your design is interrupted midstitching, it's a bother. Until recently, interrupting a design meant that you had to remove the hoop from the machine, turn the machine back on, let it go through its calibration routine, and then start the onerous task of stepping through the design until you reached exactly where the needle last stitched. Now, with auto-resume, all you need to do is turn the machine back on, reseat the hoop, and press the start button. Trust me, this is worth a lot of dollars.

I would love to include auto-resume as a must-have feature—it is *so* nice! However, auto-resume is usually available only on the top-of-the-line machines, and I don't believe that all embroiderers need the top-of-the-line machines.

But auto-resume sure is nice!

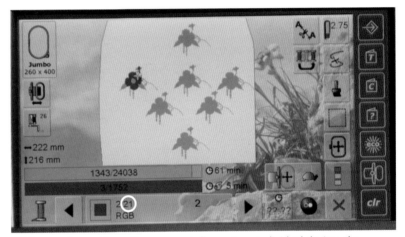

Without color sorting Because each flower is an individual design, the machine shows 21 colors, requiring 21 color changes (shown in white circle).

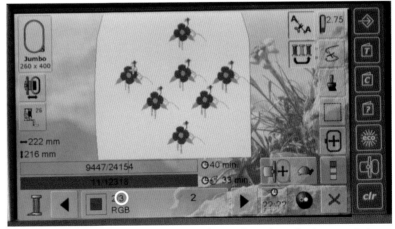

With color sorting After color sorting, the total number of colors to stitch is 3, requiring 3 color changes (shown in white circle).

Desirable: Informative Screen

The amount of information shown for each design varies by machine. Luckily, we've come a long way from the days when embroidery machines displayed only the name or number of the design. Now you can see a full picture of the design. The following are some of the useful information features available: the color you're on, how many stitches are in the current color, the total number of colors, the stitch number you're on, how many total stitches are in the design, how much time the remainder of the design will take, and a picture of where your current stitch is located. Additional desirable features on the informative screen include highlighting of the current color and picture magnification (described below).

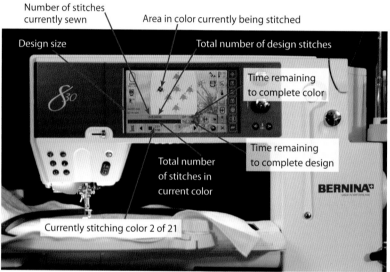

An informative screen

Desirable: Highlighting Current Color

It is useful for a machine to highlight the section that will be stitched in a specific color.

This screen shows clearly that the color currently being stitched is red. All other colors in the design are shown in gray.

Desirable: Magnification

Being able to enlarge the picture on the machine screen is useful for a variety of tasks. When you combine designs on the screen, a magnified image helps with placement. If your work is interrupted midtask, resetting your machine back to where it stopped is easier if you can magnify the stitching. Magnification is also important for placement when loading multiple designs into your machine.

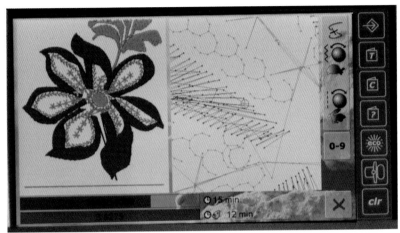

The full design and the enlarged design are shown at the same time, displaying the current stitch.

Desirable: A Big, Big, Big Bobbin

As the hoops and sewing fields get larger and larger, the designs we use also can be very large. Unfortunately, few machine manufacturers have taken this into account by providing bobbins that hold more thread. Those that do are desirable.

If you don't have an extra-large bobbin, the next best thing is to be able to use prewound bobbins, which generally hold more thread than you can wind on a standard bobbin.

Desirable: Snapshot

The top-of-the-line Brother embroidery machine has an exciting new feature: a camera that projects a live picture of the hoop onto the machine's screen. The camera aids in placement for designs requiring multiple hoopings. It transmits the picture of the previously embroidered design to the machine's screen. You load the next design into the machine and move its image around the screen, positioning it in the appropriate place in relation to the image of the previously stitched area. Being able to view the alignment of the yet-to-be-sewn design enables you to place it perfectly.

Desirable: Auto Needle Threading

Most embroidery machines include some sort of needle threader. Some work; some don't. If this is a priority for you, work with the needle threader before purchase and make sure you're comfortable with it.

Desirable: Easy-to-Use Hoop Closures

Until recently all home embroidery machine hoop closure systems were the same: a screw that reduced the size of the outer hoop when tightened.

Recently, some manufacturers have come up with alternative ways of hooping. Janome has a hoop with raised sides. You place the fabric over the sides of the hoop and snap plastic pieces over the fabric and raised sides, clamping the fabric down.

A third-party vendor, Designs in Machine Embroidery, offers the Magna-Hoop for almost every brand of machine. The Magna-Hoop consists of a metal layer that fits snugly inside the top hoop of your machine, as well as an acrylic overlay. You hoop the stabilizer in the usual way. The item to embroider goes between the metal layer and the acrylic. Strong magnets hold the two layers together with the fabric between them.

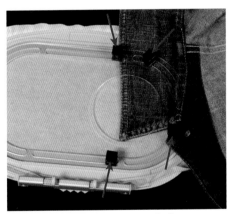

Magnets hold the top hoop with the Magna Hoop.

Another product from Designs in Machine Embroidery is the Snap-Hoop, which eliminates the screw closure. The Snap-Hoop is used as a stand-alone piece. (You don't use any of the hoops that came with your machine.) The bottom hoop of the Snap-Hoop is a flat metal layer. You place the fabric on this layer and then cover it with the Snap-Hoop's top hoop. Magnets hold the top and bottom hoops together. Not only is the screw closure tamed, but the bottom hoop is flat so that the fabric doesn't have to be draped over raised sides.

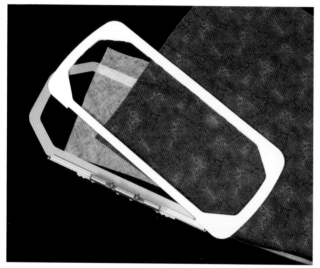

Magnets do the trick with a Snap-Hoop.

The closure of the Bernina 830's Jumbo-Hoop is particularly easy to use. After placing fabric and stabilizer in the hoop, you turn a large, easy-to-grab knob, and the hoop tightens.

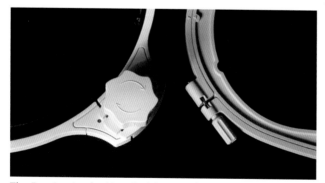

The Bernina Jumbo Hoop's tightening knob and a traditional closure

Desirable: Stepping Up

It is often necessary to step through a design without stitching. If your machine turns off in the middle of a design for any reason, you will need to get back to the place where it stopped. If your machine mis-stitches and a portion needs to be removed, when you replace the hoop in the machine you will have to step backward or forward to get your machine to the correct stitch.

Every machine has a way to move through the design to get to a specific stitch in an efficient manner. The current machines allow you to go a stitch at a time so you can end exactly where you want, and they also have the ability to fast-forward, going 10, 100, or even 1,000 stitches at a time.

One brand allows you to move to a specific stitch. For example, if your total design has 15,000 stitches and you lost power around halfway through, you can move to stitch 7,500. In another machine, you choose to "jog" through the design by clicking on a jog switch—tapping once moves the stitches singly; pressing continuously moves through the stitches at a faster rate. The machine I'm currently using has knobs to turn to step through the design. The top knob is the "turtle" knob, which steps slowly through the design in small increments. The "rabbit" knob moves much faster, up to 1,000 stitches at a time.

The rabbit and turtle knobs to step quickly or slowly through a design

Time to Embroider

Getting Started

You've got your embroidery machine. You purchased it from a dealer who provides support and training, so you know how to use the machine: how to thread it, wind the bobbin, and load the design. You've assembled all the appropriate tools. It's time to start embroidering.

If you're new to the embroidery world, you should have had basic lessons in hooping and loading a design on your machine from your dealer. Even if you've been embroidering for a while and have your own ways of hooping, read the hooping suggestions below—maybe you'll find a hint that will make life easier.

Hooping

One often overlooked skill required for excellent embroidery results is hooping—the process of preparing your fabric for the embroidery machine.

For perfect machine embroidery, the fabric must be held so that it is not pulled or puckered by the stitching. The fabric also needs to be kept in the same position relative to the hoop for the entire stitching process. If the fabric loosens or shifts, the later stitches will not align correctly with the first stitches.

The most often used way to prepare fabric for the embroidery machine is basic hooping. Basic hooping is layering fabric over stabilizer and sandwiching the two pieces between the top (called *inner* for some hoop types) and bottom (called *outer* for some hoop types) pieces of the machine's hoop. Other forms of hooping include using sticky stabilizer, using adhesives, and basting to the hoop.

Basic Hooping

1. Open the bottom (outer) section of the hoop so that the top (inner) section can fit loosely inside. The bottom (outer) hoop needs to be opened enough so that the top (inner) hoop, stabilizer, and fabric can easily fit in. Thicker fabric requires that the bottom (outer) hoop be looser than for thinner fabric.

2. Place the bottom (outer) section of the hoop on a flat surface, preferably one covered with a large cutting mat. Place the tightening screws closest to you and align one edge of the bottom (outer) hoop so it is parallel with one of the lines on the cutting mat. This ensures that all hoop edges are parallel to lines on the cutting mat.

3. Cut a piece of stabilizer large enough so that you have a minimum of 1″ overhang on all sides of the bottom (outer) hoop. Center the stabilizer on top of the bottom (outer) hoop, keeping the bottom edge of the stabilizer parallel with a straight line on the cutting mat.

4. Place the fabric on top of the stabilizer with its straight grain parallel to the edge of the stabilizer or a line on the cutting mat, unless your desired design placement requires otherwise.

5. Push down on the center of the fabric and stabilizer so that they are flat on the table. Lightly tap the corners of the fabric and stabilizer into the corners of the hoop, smoothing the center of the fabric as you tap the corners. (In Steps 3 and 4, we placed the stabilizer and fabric on top of the bottom [outer] hoop. Now we're pushing it down so that the top [inner] hoop will not move the stabilizer and fabric around when it is applied in Steps 6 and 7.)

6. Position the edge of the top (inner) hoop that is farthest from you into the corresponding edge of the bottom (outer) hoop, gently pushing the stabilizer and fabric down.

7. Push the remaining edge of the top (inner) hoop (the edge closest to you) into the bottom (outer) hoop. Hold everything in place with one hand and arm while the other hand reaches under the fabric to the tightening screw.

Holding the fabric, stabilizer, and bottom (outer) hoop, slide the top (inner) hoop into the bottom (outer) hoop.

8. Tighten as tight as possible without stripping the screw.

9. If you see places where the fabric is wrinkled or not pulled smooth, pull the fabric gently from one edge. In most fabrics you can see if you're stretching the fabric to the point that the threads curve instead of lying straight. If you see curves in the grain (either the vertical or the horizontal grain) of the fabric, release the hoop and start again.

Starting in the Right Place

Almost every embroidery project requires that the stitching for a design start in a specific spot on the fabric. Follow the instructions below to hoop the fabric so that the design ends up where you want it.

1. Using the appropriate marking tool (see Marking Pens, page 54), mark the place where you want the center of the design on the fabric.

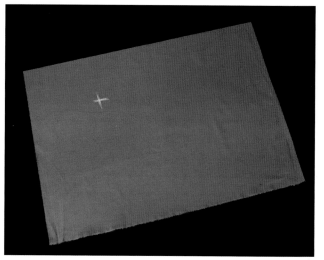

Mark the center of the design.

2. Draw lines wider than the width of the hoop and longer than the length of the hoop to create crosshairs so the center of the crosshairs is on the mark you just made in Step 1, the desired center of the design. In most cases, the vertical crosshair should be parallel with the grain of fabric.

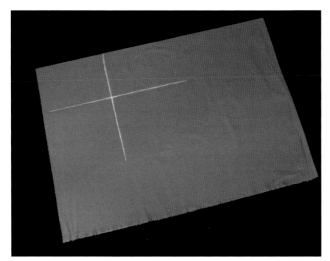

Draw lines to create crosshairs on your fabric.

3. Cut the stabilizer at least 1″ larger than the hoop, both vertically and horizontally. Place the stabilizer behind the area of the fabric you will embroider. Using a spray adhesive to hold the stabilizer in place can help, though it is not mandatory. From this point on, treat the stabilizer and fabric as a single piece.

4. Push a straight pin through the fabric and stabilizer at each end of the lines, and another pin through the center mark.

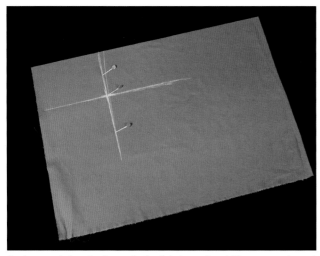

Push a straight pin through the fabric and stabilizer at each end of the lines, and another pin through the center mark.

5. Using the pins as a guide, fold the fabric vertically, right sides together, so the fold is on the vertical crosshair and you can see the pointed ends of the straight pins.

6. Place the fold of the fabric and stabilizer on the vertical alignment marks on the bottom (outer) hoop.

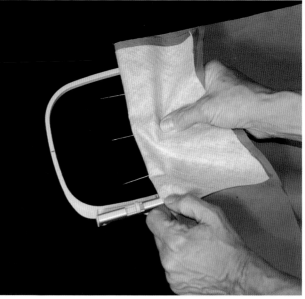

Place the folded fabric on the hoop.

NOTE *All hoops are marked at the vertical and horizontal centers. With most hoops, the vertical and horizontal centers are marked on the bottom (outer) hoop. If your hoops are marked on the top (inner) hoop, use the top (inner) hoop as a guide and make a corresponding mark on the bottom (outer) hoop.*

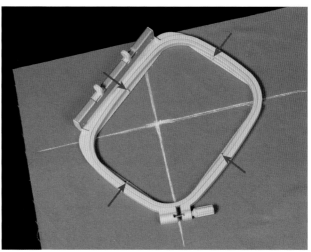

All hoops are marked at the vertical and horizontal centers.

7. Without letting the fabric move, put your hand inside the folded fabric. Push down to hold the fabric in place as you unfold the fabric. If you've done this correctly, the fold should still be on the drawn line.

Your fabric is now correctly placed for hooping. Place the top (inner) hoop on top of the fabric and gently push it down without allowing the fabric to shift. Tighten the hoop's screw.

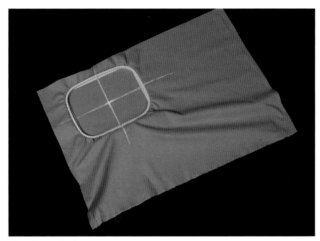

Gently push down.

Threading the Machine

Most of the embroidery machines on the market today are simple to thread; in fact, most have numbers stamped into the case to remind you of the correct threading sequence. Even so, it makes sense to spend time with the dealer learning how to thread your machine. Practicing threading with the dealer will give you confidence for when you're alone with your machine.

And while you're there, make sure you learn how to attach the hoop and start the machine stitching.

Checking Out

These steps all sound simple, and you may be thinking, "Sure, I'll remember this." But it pays to have the list typed out and taped next to your machine. Don't take it for granted that you'll remember everything on the list. Go through it *every* time you embroider. Yes, every time!

Do As I Say

Sure, starting the embroidery machine seems like a simple task: Press the start button and the machine stitches its little heart out. Imagine my embarrassment when I took home my first Bernina and couldn't make it stitch. I had it threaded, had the hoop in place, had the design loaded, and … nothing! I pressed that little button maybe 100 times.

I finally admitted defeat and placed a call to the dealer.

"I think my machine is defective. It won't stitch."

"Did you see the start button?" was the first question.

"Yes." (I was really thinking, *How dumb do you think I am?*)

"Did you hold it down for three seconds?"

And then I was thinking, *How dumb could I be?* I'd been told the three-second thing when I picked up the machine; I just hadn't thought about it again. Operator error, for sure.

So, do as I say, not as I did. When the dealer is introducing you to your machine, make sure you listen carefully for your machine's individual operating instructions. Listening carefully (and hopefully remembering) will save you a lot of feeling-stupid time.

Before You Stitch:
The Embroiderer's Checklist

Now that you have hooped the fabric, it would seem that the next step is to attach the hoop to the machine and start it stitching. However, your work will be more successful if you add an additional step, checking that everything is set up exactly right. Keep a checklist next to your sewing machine and run through it before every stitch-out. You'll eliminate the possibility for a variety of problems.

- **Is the correct design loaded?** Check to make sure that the design that is loaded is the design you want to stitch.

- **Is the design positioned correctly? Is it facing the right way?** Make sure that the design is stitching exactly where you want it on the fabric and that it isn't turned upside down or mirrored the wrong way. To be sure, mark the fabric so you can tell where the design is supposed to stitch and watch the first few stitches.

- **Is the fabric hooped properly?** Make sure that neither the fabric nor the stabilizer is folded back under the hoop. This is such an easy thing to prevent, yet it happens a lot. If you have cut the stabilizer long enough for multiple hoopings, it also might fold back under the hoop.

- **Is the right thread loaded?** Make sure you have the correct color threaded for the section you're about to stitch.

- **Does the bobbin have enough thread for the full design?** Check that the bobbin is full or at least has enough thread to get through the design.

- **Is the area around the hoop clear?** If the hoop does not have enough clearance and knocks into or hits anything while stitching, it will lose alignment. The portion of the design stitched from that point on will not be in the correct place. Check carefully behind the hoop before you begin.

- **Is anything on the fabric?** When you work on large pieces of fabric, the excess fabric can get caught under chair wheels, under the edge of the hoop, or somewhere else. Any of these situations will impede the hoop's movement—a recipe for bad stitching.

And Then You Stitch

Ah, the poetry of a smooth-running embroidery machine. I love watching a design stitch out. I love watching the machine take stitches. Turn it on, and it goes.

As much as I'd like to share a million funny stories accumulated in the hours my embroidery machine has been stitching, I can't. Today's embroidery machines are incredible. They just stitch and stitch and stitch. All my funny stories are about my mistakes, not the machines'.

Design Types

Although the most common use of the embroidery machine is to stitch directly on fabric reinforced with stabilizer, it is possible to vary the outcome by adding layers of fabric, cutting away the base fabric, stitching on stabilizer without fabric, or using other combinations.

Using a variety of embroidery designs adds interest to almost any garment. All of the designs on this jacket are on the CD included with this book.

Standard Embroidery

Most machine embroidery consists of threads stitched onto fabric, producing pictures or designs. To stitch a standard embroidery design, load the design into the machine, attach fabric hooped with stabilizer, start the

Standard embroidery

machine stitching, and change threads for the various colors. The machine produces the desired results. Practice embroidering motif designs using the six motif designs from the CD included with this book.

Appliqué Embroidery

An appliqué design incorporates an additional piece of fabric to add interest to the design. If you wish to add fabric in this manner, you must choose a design made specifically for appliqué.

Appliqué embroidery

Regular Appliqué Embroidery

Appliqué embroidery is stitched with an additional piece of appliqué fabric on top of the base fabric (as opposed to reverse appliqué embroidery, page 70, in which the appliqué fabric is underneath the base fabric) and held in place with stitches from the embroidery machine. Practice embroidering appliqué designs using the two designs from the CD included with this book.

In some cases, the embroidery designer provides a pattern for the appliqué fabric. The appliqué fabric is cut to the correct final shape, sprayed with a temporary adhesive, and then placed on the base fabric inside the placement lines. The embroidery proceeds as before.

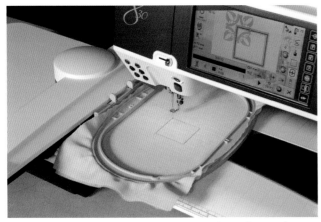

1. Hoop the fabric with stabilizer in the traditional way. The first color stitches a placement line.

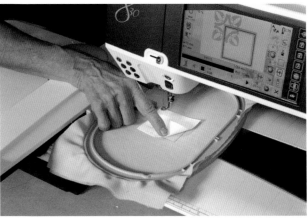

2. Cover the placement line with the appliqué fabric, cut large enough to cover the placement line. With most fabrics, the piece will remain correctly positioned. For slippery fabrics, use spray adhesive or straight pins to hold the fabric through the next color change. For small appliqués I just leave the piece on top because the first thing you do is sew it down so it doesn't have time to shift.

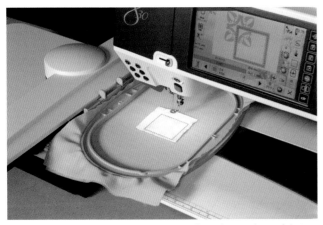

3. The next color stitch sequence attaches the appliqué fabric to the background fabric.

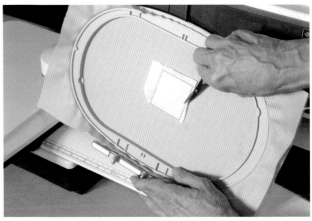

4. Remove the hoop from the machine. Do *not* remove the fabric from the hoop! Trim the appliqué fabric close to the stitch line.

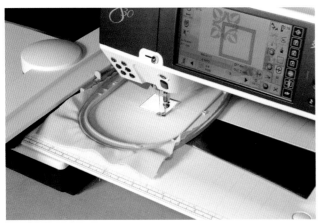

5. Attach the hoop to the machine and stitch the next color. At some point in the design, satin stitch covers the cut edge of the appliqué fabric.

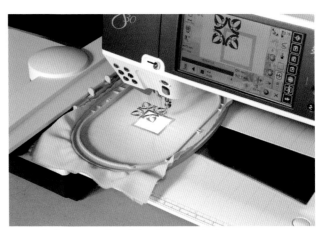

6. Stitch the remainder of the design with the remaining color changes.

Reverse embroidery appliqué
(Design included on CD: AME_REV_APPL)

Reverse Appliqué Embroidery

Reverse appliqué is similar to regular appliqué, with one major difference—the additional fabric is applied *underneath* the base fabric. Traditionally, in reverse appliqué embroidery, the secondary fabric is sheer. After the stabilizer is removed, the secondary fabric appears as an embroidered sheer panel. Practice embroidering reverse appliqué designs using the design from the CD included with this book.

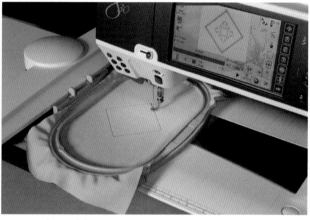

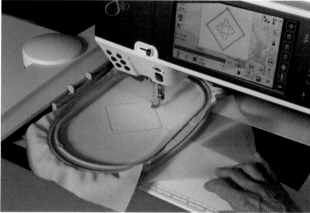

1. Hoop the stabilizer covered with the base fabric. If the secondary fabric is sheer, you must use a stabilizer that can be completely removed, such as a water-soluble or heat-away stabilizer. Stitch out the first color, the cutting line. Because the stitching will not be seen, the choice of thread for this color change is not important.

2. Slip the second fabric under the hoop. Make sure the second fabric piece is large enough to cover the area under the first stitching. In most reverse appliqué designs, the next color will stitch over the first stitching lines, attaching the appliqué fabric to the stabilizer/top (base) fabric combination. If your design does not restitch the line, step backward through the design to restitch the first color. Note that if you are using fabrics that easily wrinkle or bunch, you need to attach the reverse appliqué fabric to the stabilizer/base fabric before stitching. For these fabrics, remove the hoop from the machine without removing the fabric from the hoop. On the back of the fabric, cover the first line of stitching with the reverse appliqué fabric. Use pins or spray adhesive to hold the appliqué fabric to the stabilizer/base fabric. Replace the hoop in the machine.

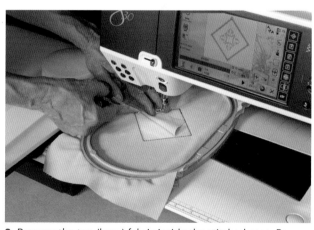

3. Remove the top (base) fabric inside the stitched area. Be careful to leave the stabilizer intact. If it is unwieldy to remove the fabric while the hoop is attached to your machine, you can remove the hoop from the machine, making sure you do not unhoop the fabric.

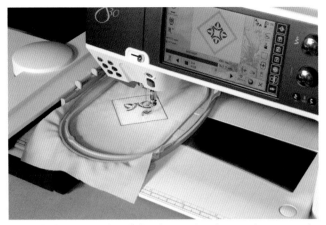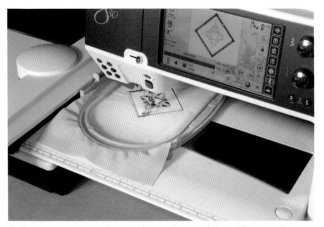

4. Stitch the remainder of the design. Stitches on the exposed stabilizer will show on the appliqué fabric after the stabilizer is removed.

5. At some point in the stitching, the machine will cover the cut edge with a satin stitch.

6. After the stitching is finished, if you used a sheer fabric for the reverse appliqué, remove the stabilizer.

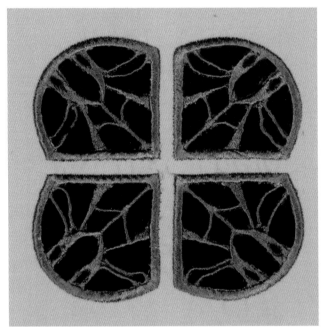

Mimicking the handwork known as Richelieu
(Design included on CD: AME_RIC1_4)

Cutwork

Mimicking the handwork known as Richelieu, cutwork creates small openings in the fabric where the cut edge is protected with a satin-stitched edging. Practice embroidering Richelieu embroidery designs using the two designs from the CD included with this book.

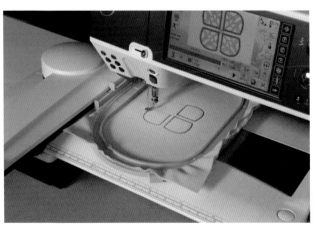

1. Choose an easily removed stabilizer such as heat-away or water-soluble. Hoop the fabric and the stabilizer. Stitch the first color, which will outline the areas to remove.

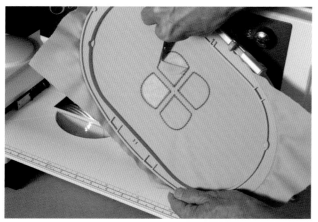

2. Leaving the fabric in the hoop, remove the hoop from the machine. Cut away all the fabric within the defined areas. Do not cut the stabilizer!

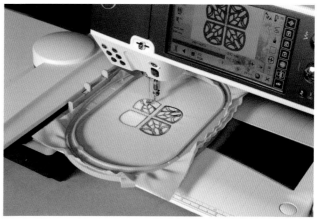

3. Replace the hoop in the machine and continue stitching. The cut edges will be covered with satin stitching in the finished design.

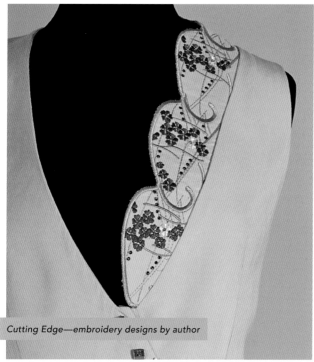

Cutting Edge—embroidery designs by author

Cut edge embroidery. The graceful edge of the lapel adds beauty and interest to this vest.

Cut Edge

Cut edge embroidery is a form of cutwork design and is created in a similar manner. Oftentimes border designs work beautifully for this type of embroidery. Practice embroidering border designs using the six designs from the CD included with this book.

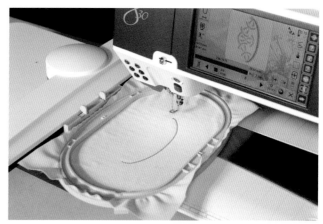

1. Hoop the stabilizer and the fabric. Stitch the first color, a line defining the area to cut.

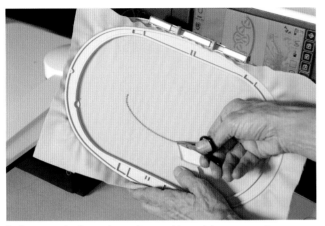

2. Remove the hoop from the machine without removing the fabric from the hoop. Being careful to cut only the fabric, clip the fabric close to the stitched edge. *Make sure you do not cut the stabilizer!*

3. Replace the hoop in the sewing machine and sew the remainder of the design. At some point during the stitching, the edge of the fabric will be covered with satin stitching.

Freestanding Lace

Freestanding lace is stitched on a water-soluble or heat-away stabilizer. After the design is stitched, the stabilizer is totally removed, leaving lace. Practice embroidering lace designs using the three designs from the CD included with this book.

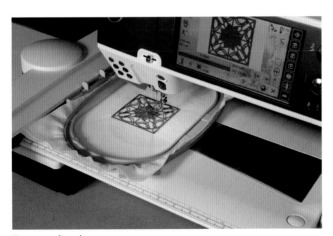

Freestanding lace

In-the-Hoop Designs

There are a variety of projects that can be constructed totally in the hoop, such as eyeglass cases, coasters, stuffed animals, and cosmetic bags. Look online for these types of projects, and because every in-the-hoop design is different, be sure to follow the designer's instructions.

Perfect Design Placement

A perfectly centered design

Although most embroiderers consider perfect design placement impossible, with a few simple steps it is easily accomplished. You *can* control exactly where an embroidery design will be stitched.

The key to perfect placement is creating and using a template made of clear material.

Supplies

- Embroidery design software and printer

- Clear acetate or comparable material to trace out a design *or* printable transparency sheets

- Ruler

- Fabric marker

- A pen or marker that shows up well on your chosen template material—ballpoint pens work well on sheet protectors

Clearly the Best

When I first started doing placement by this method, I struggled with the clear acetate templates that come with most machines. They didn't take precise lines and were hard to clean. If your template material is better behaved, by all means, use it. I prefer using the sheet protectors made for displaying documents in notebooks. They're cheap (a box of 100 is less than $12), and each protector is doubled, so you're getting 200 templates for less than the cost of a dinner out. At that price, you can toss the template when you're done. Another plus is that ballpoint pens write quite nicely on them, making clear, accurate lines.

Six Steps to Perfect Placement

1. Print a Paper Template

A paper template is a picture of the embroidery design printed the same size as the stitched design.

A. Start your software program and open a design.

B. Choose the *File* menu.

C. From the *File* menu, choose the *Print Template* option.

D. Some software programs ask whether or not to print with crosshairs. If given the choice, choose to print *with* crosshairs. Most software that does not give this option prints the crosshairs as a default. If you cannot print the crosshairs from your software, purchase another program. Crosshairs are mandatory for this process.

E. Print the paper template. Alternatively, load the printer with a printable transparency sheet and print the design on the sheet. If you are using printable transparency sheets, skip to Step 3, Choose the Design Placement (below right).

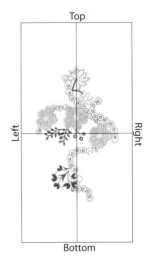

The paper template

2. Trace the Printed Template onto Clear Template Material

For this step you can use the template material that came with your machine, or you can use sheet protectors from an office supply store. If you are using printable transparency sheets, skip this step.

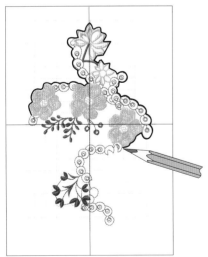

Place the clear template material over the paper template. Alignment of the clear sheet with the edge of the printout is not important. Trace around the edges of the design and the center crosshairs, producing a *clear* template.

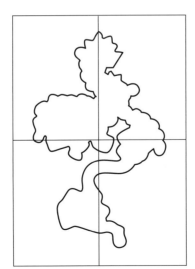

The clear template

3. Choose the Design Placement

Whether you are stitching on a quilt block, a constructed garment, a pillowcase, fabric for a garment, or any other project, the clear template allows complete control of the design placement. The following example shows this technique on a purchased jean jacket.

Place the jacket on a smooth surface with the jacket back facing up. Smooth the fabric to produce as flat a surface as possible.

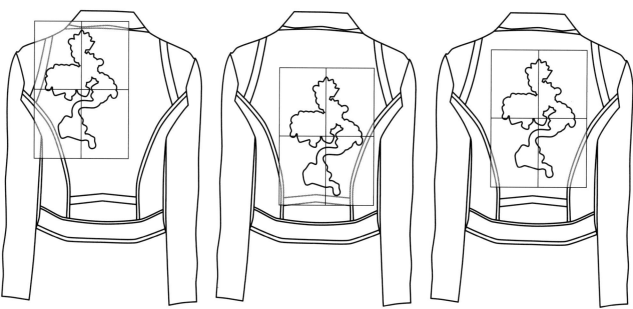

Move the template to find the most pleasing placement.

4. Transfer the Crosshairs onto the Fabric

A. After arranging the template so the outline of the design is in the desired position, place a ruler next to the vertical crosshair line as shown.

B. Using a fabric marker, mark the fabric above and below the template, extending the crosshair line onto the fabric.

C. Align the ruler with the horizontal crosshair line and mark the right and left sides, continuing the line onto the fabric.

D. Remove the clear template to show the 4 lines.

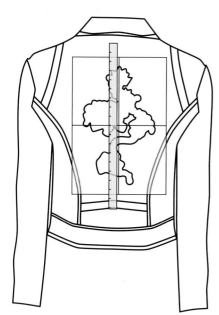

Place a ruler next to the vertical crosshair line.

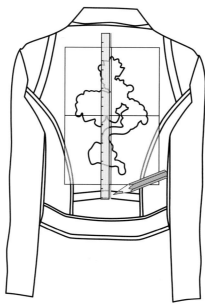

Mark the fabric above and below the template.

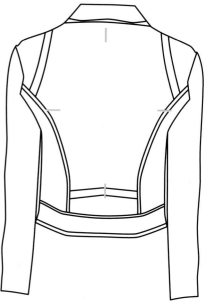

The four lines

E. Place a ruler next to the horizontal lines. Using the fabric marker, connect the lines. Repeat for the vertical lines.

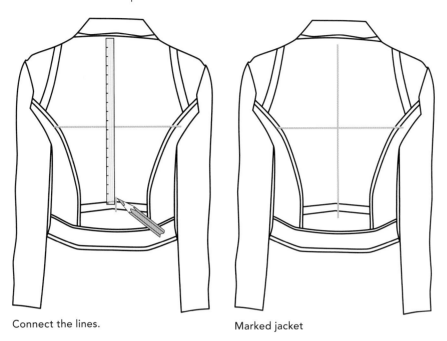

Connect the lines.   Marked jacket

5. Hoop the Fabric

All embroidery hoops have marks in the vertical and horizontal center that correspond to the crosshair marks (see Note, page 65).

Hoop the jacket with the cross-hairs on the fabric lined up with the vertical and horizontal marks on the hoop (see Starting in the Right Place, page 64). The hooping does not need to be perfect. The marks on the fabric can be as much as ½˝ away from the marks on the hoop, as long as the drawn line is equidistant from both corresponding marks on the hoop. Embroidery machines allow minor adjustments before stitching.

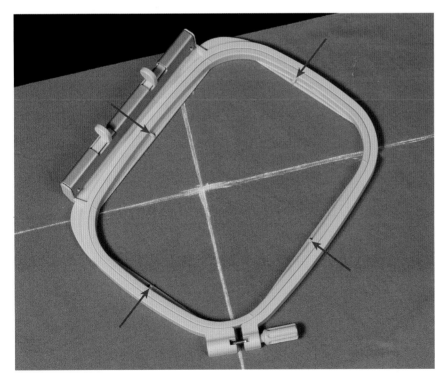

Vertical and horizontal hoop marks

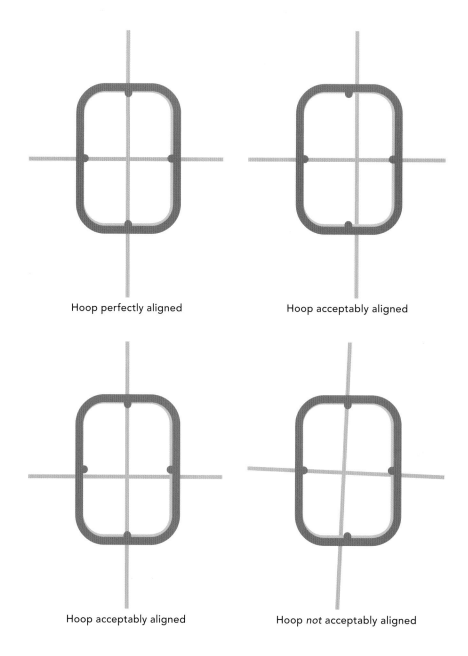

Hoop perfectly aligned

Hoop acceptably aligned

Hoop acceptably aligned

Hoop *not* acceptably aligned

The crosshairs don't have to line up perfectly with the vertical and horizontal centers as long as the crosshairs are parallel with the center marks.

6. Stitch the Design

A. Place the hoop in the machine. The needle, when centered, should be over the intersection of the marked crosshairs. Move the needle to align with the design center, if necessary, using the adjustment indicators on your machine.

B. Following the color change chart that came with the design, stitch the design.

Ah, Perfection

It amazes me how easy it is to get a design exactly where you want it. Until I learned this method I had thought perfect placement was an impossible task. Now I can embroider a design exactly where I want it every time.

Combining Designs

There are times when embroidery designs the size of even your largest hoop are not sufficient. You may want to fill larger spaces with swoops and swirls of color to add texture and interest over the body of your newest project. In these cases, rehooping becomes a necessary skill.

Once you've conquered precise placement (see Perfect Design Placement, pages 74–78), combining designs is easy. You can use a design that is created to be stitched in multiple hoopings, or you can create your own megadesign by combining your choice of embroidery designs. We'll cover both options.

Using a Design Created for Multiple Hoopings

1. Print the Templates

If you're stitching a design that was made specifically for multiple hoopings, print out the template of the entire finished design. The sample below is the design Regency Living Large from Bullard Designs. While you have the printer and software running, print the paper templates for each of the 4 design components (together, they make up the complete design).

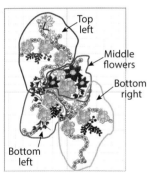

Top left

Middle flowers

Bottom right

Bottom left

Printout of the entire design

2. Trace the Templates

Make a clear template for each of the individual designs by tracing around the printed paper templates for the individual designs (see Step 2, Trace the Printed Template onto Clear Template Material, page 75). Be sure to trace the center lines and alignment marks.

Make a clear template for each of the individual designs.

3. Place the Designs

If you are making a garment, place the garment pattern piece on the fabric and trace around the edges. Otherwise, cut out a piece of fabric large enough for the finished project. In the case of Regency Living Large, a minimum of 15″ × 20″ is required.

Using the paper printout of the entire design, decide where to place the finished design. Shift the printout around the pattern until you like the location.

The instructions with the multi-hooped embroidery design indicate the design stitching order—in this case, top left, bottom right, bottom left, and then the middle flowers.

4. Draw the Crosshairs on the Fabric

Place the clear template for the first stitch-out (top left) on top of the paper layout. Make sure your drawing of the outline of the top left design is over the corresponding part of the printout.

Hold the clear template in place. If any portion of the template is overlapping the fabric and not totally on top of the paper pattern, use a bit of

Align the clear template for the first design stitch-out over the printed pattern of the full design.

masking tape to secure the clear template to the fabric. Otherwise, hold the clear template as you carefully slip the printout away without moving the clear template. Place a ruler next to the vertical center line of the clear template. Using an air erasable or chalk marker, draw a line next to the ruler, above and below the clear template, on the fabric. Repeat on the horizontal center line of the clear template.

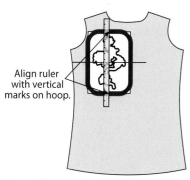

Align ruler with vertical marks on hoop.

Draw a line on the fabric above and below the clear template.

Remove the clear template, connect the top and bottom vertical lines on the fabric, and then connect the left and right horizontal lines.

5. Hoop the Fabric

Hoop the fabric with the vertical and horizontal lines aligned with the marks on the sides, top, and bottom of your hoop (see Starting in the Right Place, page 64).

6. Stitch the First Design

Stitch Design 1 (the first design component) using the appropriate color changes.

7. Mark for the Second Design

A. Place the clear template for the second design (Design 2) on top of the paper template of the full, assembled design.

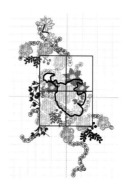

Place the clear template for the second design on the paper printout of the complete design.

B. With the Design 2 clear template on top of the full design paper printout, trace enough of the design you have already stitched (Design 1) to be able to orient the clear template on the fabric stitch-out. (Shown here in red.)

Trace enough of the design for orientation.

C. Place the clear template over the fabric, matching the section traced from Design 1 over the corresponding part of the stitch-out of Design 1.

Place the clear template on the fabric.

D. Place a ruler next to the crosshairs for Design 2 and mark them as you did for Design 1.

E. Remove the clear template and connect the crosshairs.

8. Hoop and Stitch the Second Design

Hoop and stitch the second design using the new set of crosshairs, as you did for Design 1, Steps 5 and 6 (at left).

9. Repeat the Steps with the Remaining Designs

Repeat Steps 7 and 8 (above) until you are finished.

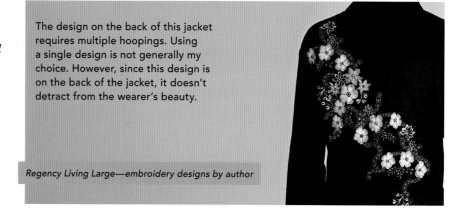

The design on the back of this jacket requires multiple hoopings. Using a single design is not generally my choice. However, since this design is on the back of the jacket, it doesn't detract from the wearer's beauty.

Regency Living Large—embroidery designs by author

Creating Your Own Multi-Hooped Design

Perhaps you have a vision of combining a variety of designs stitched close together to produce the look of a single large design.

First choose the designs to combine and print a template for each design.

1. Print and Trace the Templates

Print paper templates of your chosen designs. Print out multiple copies of the paper template for any design you will use more than once in the final project. On a large piece of paper, arrange the paper templates as you would like to stitch them. Tape the templates to the background sheet.

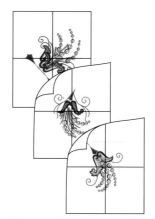

Arrange the paper templates.

2. Combine the Designs in Your Software

In your embroidery software, combine as many of the designs as will fit in a single hooping into a single design in the same arrangement as your combined designs. Print the paper template for the design you've just created.

Using techniques similar to those described in Using a Design Created for Multiple Hoopings (pages 79 and 80), place your traced clear templates over the stitched designs to guide subsequent design placement.

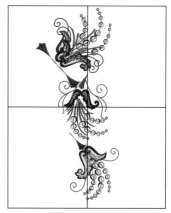

Print a paper template for the combined designs.

Continuous Line of Designs

Continuous lines of designs are an easy way to add punch to a wearable art project. A long line of a repeated design almost always looks graceful. Luckily, stitching continuous lines is easily accomplished.

Choose a design created for continuous stitching or stitch multiple copies of a design of your choice. Either way, the process is easy.

Some brands of embroidery machines offer continuous hoops. They work well, but most of them allow the design to be stitched only close to and parallel to the edge of the fabric. The following instructions (pages 83 and 84) allow placement of a continuous-line design anywhere on a project.

Purchased Continuous-Line Designs

When a digitizer creates a design to be repeated and used as a continuous line, he or she will include alignment marks. Alignment marks are small X- or L-shaped marks included in all sections of a multi-hooped design. The mark or marks will stitch close to the edge of the design. After one section is stitched, the first color change of the next section will be a repeat of the X- or L-shaped mark. If this stitching of the mark is exactly on top of the first, the alignment will be correct. The alignment marks simplify the process of stitching a continuous line.

The beauty of an elaborate design stitched in a continuous line

Light & Lacy—embroidery designs by author

Continuous lines

Adornments—embroidery designs by author

The steps below are a modification of the perfect placement process (see Six Steps to Perfect Placement, page 75).

1. Create a Clear Template

Using your embroidery software, print a paper template of your design. Trace the template onto an acetate sheet. Make sure you trace over the alignment marks and the center crosshairs.

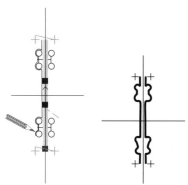

Trace the printed paper template onto a clear sheet. Don't forget to trace the alignment marks and the crosshairs.

2. Mark the Center Line

Decide where the repeated designs will be stitched and where the first repeat will be located. Draw a line on the fabric corresponding to what will be the long center of the line of designs.

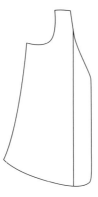

Draw the center line of the designs.

3. Mark for the First Hooping

Position the clear template so the center line of the crosshair is over the line marked on the fabric.

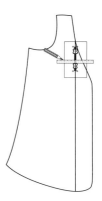

Position the clear template on top, over the drawn line.

4. Draw the Horizontal Placement Line

Place a ruler next to the horizontal crosshair. Mark the fabric, continuing the crosshair line onto the fabric on both sides of the template. Remove the clear template and connect the horizontal lines.

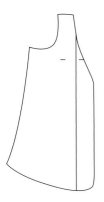

Removing the template reveals the two marks. Connect the two marks to create a crosshair.

5. Hoop and Stitch

Hoop the fabric with the marked lines corresponding to the marked centers on the sides of the hoop (see Starting in the Right Place, page 64). Stitch the design. Note that the alignment marks are also stitched in place.

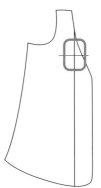

Hoop the fabric.

6. Prepare for the Next Design

A. Place the clear template so that the top of the traced design connects with the bottom of the previously stitched design. The traced alignment marks should lie on top of the stitched alignment marks and the long center line should be continuous. I don't emphasize exactness here, however, because you can actually stray a tad and adjust when your hoop is in the machine.

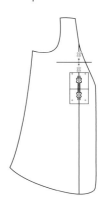

Place the template so that the traced design connects with the stitched design.

B. Mark the horizontal crosshair as you did for the first stitching.

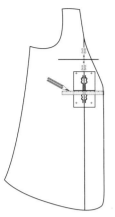

Place a ruler next to the horizontal crosshair and continue the line onto the fabric.

C. Align the hoop with the newest marks and hoop the fabric.

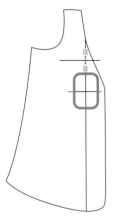

Hoop the fabric.

7. Place the Hoop in the Sewing Machine

Move your machine to the first stitch. If the needle is not over the center of the alignment mark, use the adjustment indicator arrow markers to realign the embroidery. Keep moving the embroidery until the needle is exactly over the middle of the crosshairs. Move to the second stitch. The needle should be over the end line of the alignment mark. If not, move the embroidery design. Continue adjusting until the stitches of the alignment mark are over the stitches of the previously stitched crisscross.

8. Stitch the Next Design

Following the color changes for the design, stitch the design, including the next set of alignment marks.

9. Repeat Steps 6-8 until Finished

Making sure you keep the hoop centered over the drawn center line, repeat Steps 6–8 (pages 83 and 84) until your line is the desired length.

Be All You Can Be— Be a Designer!

When you create your own continuous-line designs, the process is basically the same as with Purchased Continuous-Line Designs (page 82), but you won't have alignment marks. You choose where the next design goes in relation to the previous design. Mark the crosshairs the same way as with purchased designs.

Place the design so it parallels the curve of the pattern piece.

Following a Curve

The steps to create a curved line are similar to those for a straight continuous line. Instead of placing the vertical crosshair on a drawn straight line, place the designs so their edges are parallel to the curve of the edge of the garment pattern piece.

Notice that the design, following the curved edge of the vest, draws the eye up and to the left.

Dragon's Treasure Chest— embroidery designs by author

Designs follow the edge of the collar on this camel vest.

Bold and Beautiful (mini design set)—embroidery designs by author

I designed this vest for a runway, using large designs that could be seen from a distance.

Stitching Multiple Designs in a Single Hooping

When stitching multiple small designs, hooping for each design can waste stabilizer. You can stitch multiple designs using a single hooping of stabilizer in a large hoop by following these steps.

1. Using a fabric marker, mark on the fabric where you want the center of the design to be stitched.

2. Using your largest hoop, hoop the stabilizer only.

3. Load the single design.

4. Use the machine's basting function to stitch the outline of the design in a basting stitch.

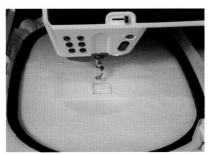

The basted outline stitched on the rectangle

5. Remove the hoop from the machine, *leaving the stabilizer in the hoop.*

6. Arrange the fabric over the mark indicating the proposed center of the design in the middle of the basted outline on the stabilizer. Use either spray adhesive or straight pins to hold the fabric to the stabilizer.

The fabric is pinned so the center target for embroidery is centered over the basted rectangle.

7. Replace the hoop in the machine and embroider the design.

Embroider the design.

8. Remove the hoop from the machine, *leaving the stabilizer in the hoop.*

9. Cut the fabric off the stabilizer. Reach behind the fabric and cut a hole in the stabilizer around the design, releasing the fabric from the hoop. The stabilizer remains in the hoop with a hole where the first design was removed.

The hooped stabilizer after the first design has been removed

10. Replace the hoop in the machine. Using the machine's design placement arrows, move the design so it will not stitch over the hole.

Position the design so it will stitch over a clear area.

11. Repeat the steps. Follow Step 1 and Steps 4–9 to complete the second design.

12. Follow Steps 10 and 11 to complete the remaining designs.

Covering Fabric with Designs

Regular Patterns

To create a regular pattern, copy your garment's pattern piece onto tracing paper. After deciding the distance between designs, draw a grid on the traced pattern. The spacing between the lines of the grid should correspond to the distance you've chosen between designs. The size of the grid depends on the size of the designs and how much fabric you are covering. Most of my grids range from 2″ to 4″.

Fold on the horizontal and vertical lines, and cut a small snip at each intersection, leaving a diamond cutout. Place the traced pattern on the fabric and make a mark through the cut.

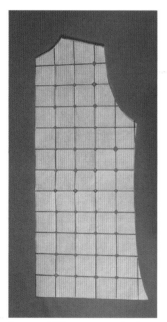  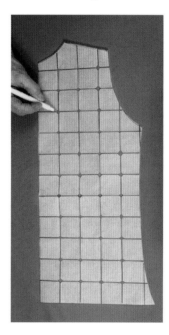

Draw grid lines, cut at the intersections, and then mark the fabric.

Embroider at each mark, using the method described in Stitching Multiple Designs in a Single Hooping (page 85).

Irregular Patterns

For irregularly patterned areas, arrange multiple designs in your largest hoop and stitch (see Creating Your Own Multi-Hooped Design, page 81).

Because of the shape of the pattern piece and the shape of the hoop, there are often empty spaces. After stitching, examine the work carefully. Does any part look empty? Using the method described in Stitching Multiple Designs in a Single Hooping, Steps 1–9 (page 85), fill the empty space with a design.

Putting It All Together

My Design Process

So far this book has been filled with technical information, the elements of design, the principles of design, the embroidery tool kit, and steps for perfecting embroidery. The remainder of this book explains how I work. You can work exactly as I do or use any part of the suggestions.

I'm not the kind of person who can visualize a work of art and have it flow directly into a finished piece. The way I work starts with something that inspires me. Then I gather the materials, see how they look together, and start to compose. Most of the time my first try at a project doesn't look anything like the vision in my head. What's worse, my first try often doesn't look good. I have to change elements, rearrange sections, modify the color palette, replace materials with different options. The most important steps in my design process are the evaluation and reworking steps.

Inspiration

I don't have one particular method for creating a project. Sometimes I start with a fabric; other times an embroidery design or set of designs calls out to me. A combination of colors will appeal to me. The shadows on the wall will inspire a silhouette. Often, I see a pattern I like. Inspiration is everywhere.

Fabric inspiration

Fabric-Based Inspiration

Sometimes a fabric will sing to me. It might warble a tune from the shelves of my stash or belt out a melody when I'm wandering down the aisles of a fabric store. (I have to admit that most fabrics that call from the fabric store demand a year or two or three in my closet before they're ready to be included in a project.) Anyway, however it happens, the fabric is singing, demanding a place in a project.

My process is to take out the fabric and find a variety of items that look right with it. I spread everything out on my sewing table: the fabric, coordinating fabric, threads, and embellishments.

On the first day it's all good. I love everything there. Every time I walk by it, ideas dance in my head. It's on the second day that some of the pieces seem out of place. That little skein of thread is obviously the wrong color. How did I not notice that yesterday? The bouclé knit doesn't go. What was I thinking? It's much too heavy to go with the delicate base fabric.

After several days of this, the pile has dwindled to a few choice pieces—they're the ones. This is the foundation for my next project.

Pattern-Based Inspiration

As a purveyor of sewing patterns, it is good business when I use one of the patterns I sell. When a pattern intrigues me, I start with that pattern and go from there, as described in Fabric-Based Inspiration (above).

Pattern as inspiration

Design-Based Inspiration

Either a new design permeates my brain and bothers me until I design a new design set, or I become fixated on one of my older designs. This is it! I *must* use this design and its companions.

Embroidery design inspiration

After a design plants itself in my brain, I start searching the fabric closets. I move all the fabrics that seem like a good match for the design to the sewing table. Sometimes I'll pull out the most likely one and give it a test drive in the embroidery machine. Some fabrics are sent back to the closet fairly quickly; others are embroidered. Eventually one stands out.

Challenge-Based Inspiration

Sometimes a practical challenge motivates a new approach. For example, I wanted to add a stripe of embellished fabric to a ruana—a square fabric wrap with a keyhole cut out to accommodate the head. It is common for the wrong side of a ruana to show as the wearer tosses an end of the square over the shoulder. The challenge was to add the stripe in such a way that the wrong side looked neat. *Voilà!* A new technique and a new garment.

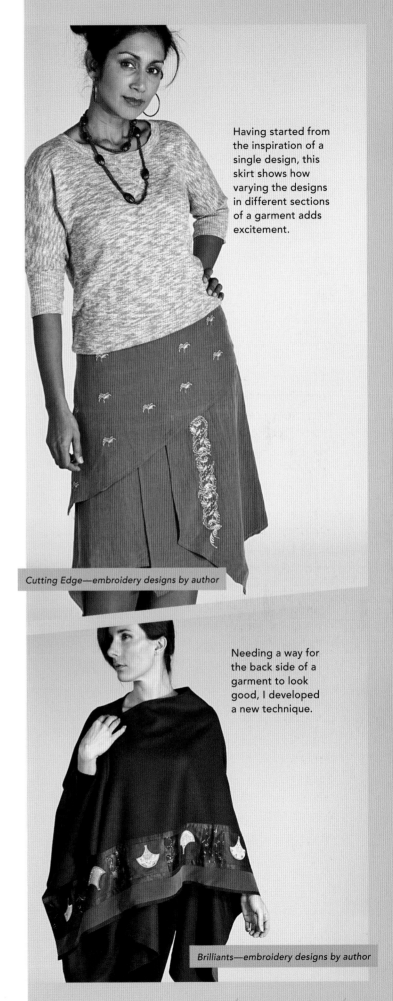

Having started from the inspiration of a single design, this skirt shows how varying the designs in different sections of a garment adds excitement.

Cutting Edge—embroidery designs by author

Needing a way for the back side of a garment to look good, I developed a new technique.

Brilliants—embroidery designs by author

Vision-Based Inspiration

On occasion, a picture will appear in my brain, a visual idea. Recently the image of a checkerboard of fabrics had been floating around, teasing me. One night, as I lay in bed, small squares of dupioni silk in a variety of colors appeared to me. I could see the beauty of adding embroidery to a smattering of the blocks. So I wouldn't forget, I pulled out my journal and made notes.

Experimentation with squares of dupioni and embroidery came together in a finished piece.

Assignment-Based Inspiration

As a writer and embroidery designer, I am occasionally assigned a specific task. One month I was asked to embellish a purchased garment. Another month the assignment was to create a garment using cutwork designs. In most cases, the assignment stretches my creativity. To come up with something exciting and unique that meets these constraints is a challenge.

Example-Based Inspiration

I'm often taken by the sheer beauty of a blouse, a skirt, a quilt, or any other wonderful piece of art. I am lucky to live in an area where I am surrounded by talented and creative people. Several years ago, a friend and fellow sewing guild member wore a blouse she had created using chiffon layered over a solid fabric. She embroidered on the top layer in some places and the bottom in others. She used the same design on both fabrics, keeping the look coherent. The change from over to under the chiffon added interest. It took almost four years before that seed began to sprout and I used the concept. My blouse doesn't look anything like hers. Inspiration doesn't mean copying.

A purchased blouse with appliquéd designs

Crystal Treasures—embroidery designs by author

Chiffon layered over silk charmeuse. The embroidery on one panel is through both layers, on the next through the bottom layer only.

Starry Night—embroidery designs by author

Making Choices

Of course inspiration is just the beginning. Once you have your starting place, then you need to actually work. The next step is to choose what goes with your initial piece.

Design Placement

A question that I hear a lot is, "How do you know where to put your designs?" The answer is that I don't. I experiment. There are several ways to do this.

Doodling

The method I use most often for choosing design placement is to draw a rough copy of the line drawing of the garment pattern in a large size and duplicate that five times on five pieces of paper.

Five line drawings

Then I doodle. Sometimes I use pencil, and other times I draw with colored pens. Soon I have a feel for what parts of the garment to cover with designs. I can visualize a design set or other embellishments. I can see if adding insets of other fabrics will add to the overall effect. I can see what shapes to make each of my doodles, the shapes of the designs.

I fill one sheet and study it. Would minor changes help? What if I make lines instead of individual motifs? What if I connect the motifs with couching (stitching over a heavy thread)? Should I cluster more things around the neck? Go for symmetry? Asymmetry? And so on. Now I'm ready to start on the second line drawing using some of these ideas. I keep going until I've filled all five pages. One of the pages will be a good starting point for a project.

When I teach classes, one of the exercises is for the students to make five line drawings of their garments. Everyone grumbles about this. "Why five? What's it for?" they ask. "Won't one do?"

The answer is that one *won't* do. If you have only one line drawing and you fill it with something halfway presentable, you will stop there. If you have five copies, even if your first try is presentable, you will go on from there and try something new. Almost always you will make improvements and one of the later pages will outshine the first try.

Using Cutouts

After you've chosen the fabric and design, use cutouts of the design to audition arrangements: Print a template or draw a full-size version of the design. Stack four or five sheets of paper topped with the template or drawing. Cut all the layers around the edges of the design. You now have multiple versions of the design.

Place the fabric on your sewing table and trace around the edges of a garment pattern piece with a fabric marker.

Arrange the design cutouts within the outline of the pattern piece until you're happy with the arrangement. The designs are easily moved to find the best placement.

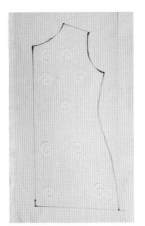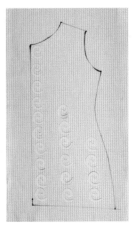

Move the cutouts of the design until you love the arrangement.

Choosing Thread Colors

 Once the fabric is on my sewing table I have to choose the colors for my embroidery. I'm very particular about my color combinations, and often what I am sure will be beautiful is not. I *always* test my colors. I stitch out the design using the threads I've chosen. Sometimes just changing the thread from one place in the design to another perfects a look. Sometimes I replace one of the threads with a different color choice.

Changing where a color stitches can change the look of a design.

After picking colors, I stitch the design. And then I stitch it again, changing where I use each of the colors. Sometimes I have to switch one of the chosen colors to something different. Until I stitch, I don't know what works best. Stitching the design multiple times, with varying color combinations, is mandatory for me. I do this for *every* project. Stitch the design over and over until you *love* the arrangement of the colors.

Adding Fabrics or Other Embellishments

I choose embellishments and fabrics to add to a project in the same manner as I choose thread colors. I place ribbons, yarns, beads, and even other fabrics around the base fabric and leave them on my sewing table for a few days. Some items speak to me; some seem totally wrong.

Inspiration Begets Choice Begets Inspiration

My working method is experiment based. I try things and see how they look. Then I try some more. Sometimes one combination gives birth to new ideas, which then inspire even more changes. Doing this preplanning is the most important part of the process.

My creative process isn't regimented. The listing here is just a sampling of what inspires me. The shadows under a tree can start my mind going. A combination of colors, the fall fashion week website, a visit to a mall—all of these can get me going.

And inspiration is just the first step. I work in a mode of continual experimentation.

One important element in my process is evaluation. I study other people's work and dissect it. If I love a dress, what impresses me most? How do the colors affect me? Is the overall effect calming? Exciting?

For my own work, I think I've perfected the art of editing, as defined by my favorite design mentor, Tim Gunn. I can look at my work and see what looks good and what doesn't. I spot sections of the work that look out of balance, uncoordinated, or wrong.

I know I've already said it, but I'm going to say it again: *Testing is critical to my creative process.* I test to choose the best tools, to see if specific fabrics look good together, to determine design placement, and even for color coordination.

Construction

Regardless of what you are making, the basic construction process is the same.

The Construction Process

1. Trace the Pattern onto the Fabric

I'm often asked if I embroider before or after I've made my garments. My method is to embroider before I even cut the fabric. I lay the pattern pieces on the fabric and trace around each piece. This allows me to embroider to the edge of the fabric. If somehow or other my embroidery is a teeny tiny bit off grain, I can adjust the pattern so it is in the exact right place in relation to the embroidery.

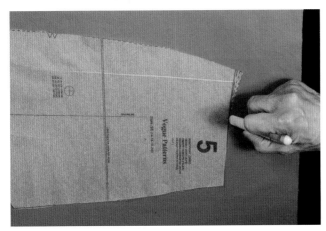

Trace around the edges of the pattern.

2. Embroider

After tracing the pattern, stabilize and embroider using the techniques described in Time to Embroider (pages 63–67).

3. Remove the Stabilizer

Remove the stabilizer.

- Machine wash the fabric for wash-away stabilizers (first tear away large pieces if using that type of stabilizer).

- Use an iron to remove heat-aways.

- Trim cut-away stabilizers close to the embroidery.

- Trim all threads.

4. Cut Out the Pattern

Place the pattern pieces on the embroidered fabric and cut around them, making sure you're comfortable with where the designs fall within the pattern piece.

Symmetrical Sections

If your design includes sections where the embroidery will be symmetrical, for example, the right and left fronts of a blouse, you'll need to take extra steps when cutting. First, place the pattern on the embroidered fabric for the first front, making sure the designs are appropriately placed on the pattern space. Cut. Then place the cut piece on top of the fabric for the next section, right sides together, making sure each design on the first piece matches a design on the uncut piece. Using the first piece as a pattern, cut out the second.

5. Add Additional Embellishment

After the fabric is cut into pattern pieces, arrange the pieces in the positions they'll occupy in the finished project. Now you can evaluate the embroidery and decide how much, if any, additional embroidery or embellishment to add.

Would it help to add lines to frame the embroidery or to make the seams more prominent? Would the addition of beading or feathers or yarns add to the overall look? If so, choose which embellishments need to be added before construction and which after.

6. Construct the Project

Following the pattern instructions, create your project.

Summary

Preplanning takes a substantial amount of time. Embroidery can also be quite time-consuming. The actual construction usually goes quickly.

For me, editing takes place at every step of a project. On occasion, I examine the project and don't like a part of it. When that happens I change it. I might have to replace a panel with one that has more embroidery or different embroidery. I have been known to add dividing lines made of Ultrasuede or bias tape (purchased or self-made). Another easy fix is to add more embroidery—that usually helps. One of the biggest design mistakes I find is lonely designs sprinkled around a shirt or jacket. So often, more is better.

For blouses and jackets, the choice of buttons is an important consideration. Most of my pieces are so heavily embellished that I choose discreet buttons. Zippers are becoming more important in design— it's becoming a design element to have the zipper tape visible, so the choice of zipper can make or break a finished piece.

The most important advice I can give is for you to enjoy the process. If you are in a hurry or if you are sewing to save money, this type of embellishment is not for you. This type of work takes time, but the results are worth it. Breathe deeply, slow down, and enjoy the process!

The Design Editing Checklist

Here are some questions to ask yourself as you are working:

- Do you like the overall look of the piece?
- Do the colors work in harmony?
- Does any one color stand out?
- If so, are you happy with that?
- If all colors have equal weight, are you happy with that?
- What is the mood set with the colors?
- Is this the mood you wanted?
- If not, what colors would you have to change to create a different mood?
- Does the piece look heavy or light? Is that okay with you?
- Are the elements on the piece balanced?
- Does any element stand out?
- If so, are you happy with that?
- Are the proportions pleasing to your eye?
- Is any spot empty looking?
- Is the piece too busy looking? Is there anywhere for your eye to rest?
- Is the piece interesting enough? If not, what can you do to add interest?
- Does the eye move around the piece?
- How does the garment look when the person wearing it moves?
- How are the proportions?
- Does the garment flatter the wearer?

About the Author

Award-winning Bobbi Bullard is known for her wearable art that's really wearable!

Bobbi Bullard has been a prominent name in the machine embroidery world since 1996. She is known for her unique and beautifully crafted embroidery designs as well as her style in using them in wearable art and quilting projects. Those who learn from her enjoy her clear-headed approach to design, her humor, and her ability to make complex concepts simple.

Bobbi has developed unique methods for individualizing garments with a variety of embellishment techniques ranging from spray dyeing to rubber stamping to stenciling to an array of bling techniques. Her work extends from wearable art to art quilts.

She has been entertaining and amazing sewing enthusiasts for years, teaching around the country, inspiring people wherever she goes.

Bobbi's work has been seen in *Quiltmaker, Belle Armoire, Total Embellishment Newsletter,* the American Sewing Guild's *Notions, Threads, Haute Handbags, Stitches* magazine, and more. She writes recurringly for *Designs in Machine Embroidery.* In addition, she has been featured on the sewing television show *It's Sew Easy.* Her work has taken ribbons in the wearable art category at the Pacific International Quilt Festival and the Sulky Challenge and has been seen in a variety of other nationally ranked quilt shows.

Visit Bobbi's website at www.bullarddesigns.com for the designs used in this book (other than those on the attached bonus CD), and for needles, stabilizers, and scissors. Other items are readily available from your local sewing machine dealer.

Great Titles and Products

from C&T PUBLISHING and stashBOOKS.

Londa Rohlfing
Sweatshirt
Transformations

Sew
Jackets,
Vests &
Hoodies

8 Projects
from Cozy
to Elegant

Thread Magic Garden

Create Enchanted Quilts
with Thread Painting
& Intuitive Appliqué

Ellen Anne Eddy

B A B Y
T I M E S

24 Handmade Treasures for Baby & Mom

Abbey Lane Quilts

Quilts,
Soft Toys,
Gifts

Ultimate 3-in-1
COLOR
TOOL
Updated 3rd Edition

816 Colors with CMYK, RGB & HEX Formulas!

24 Color Cards with
Numbered Swatches

5 Color Plans for
Each Color

2 Value Finders
Red & Green

Joen Wolfrom

Hat Shop

25 Projects to Sew,
from Practical
to Fascinating

DESIGN
Collective

Compiled by Susanne Woods

Bags
the Modern Classics

Sue Kim

❋ Clutches, Hobos, Satchels & More ❋
19 Projects • 75+ Bags

Available at your local retailer or **www.ctpub.com** *or* **800-284-1114**

For a list of other fine books from C&T Publishing, visit our website
to view our catalog online.

C&T PUBLISHING, INC.

P.O. Box 1456
Lafayette, CA 94549
800-284-1114

Email: ctinfo@ctpub.com
Website: www.ctpub.com

C&T Publishing's professional photography services are now available to
the public. Visit us at www.ctmediaservices.com.

Tips and Techniques can be found at www.ctpub.com > Consumer
Resources > Quiltmaking Basics: Tips & Techniques for Quiltmaking & More

For quilting supplies:

COTTON PATCH

1025 Brown Ave.
Lafayette, CA 94549
Store: 925-284-1177
Mail order: 925-283-7883

Email: CottonPa@aol.com
Website: www.quiltusa.com

Note: Fabrics shown may not be currently available, as fabric
manufacturers keep most fabrics in print for only a short time.